Florals

For All Seasons

Published by

krause publications

700 East State Street • Iola, WI 54990-0001
715/445-2214 • FAX: 715/445-4087   www.krause.com

Please call or write for our free catalog of publications. Our toll-free number to place an order or obtain a free catalog is 800-258-0929 or please use our regular business telephone 715-445-2214.

Library of Congress Catalog Number 2001096286
ISBN 0-87349-404-0

Printed in the United States of America

Acknowledgments

There are numerous people who helped make this book possible. A huge "thank you" to the designers who offered their amazing ideas—Sherry Bartman, Jane Davis, Diane Flowers, Lisa Galvin, Gail Gregor, Debba Haupert, Lauren Johnston, Kathy Kromer, Chris Malone, Kristy McNeil, Richard Nichols, Andi Rothenberg, Elaine Schmidt, Kathryn Severns, Edwin R. Smith, Ritsu Waggoner, and Kim Wakefield—not to mention the manufacturers that generously provided product and projects, Syndicate Sales (thank you, Kristy) and Dow Chemical Company (a special thanks to Sharon Currier). Finally, it is necessary to acknowledge graphic designer Marilyn Hochstatter, cover designer Kim Schierl, and photographer Bob Best for all of their outstanding work, dedication, and patience.

Welcome to
Florals For All Seasons

Flowers make any house feel like a home. They are that finishing touch that makes a room feel complete and inviting. This book will show you everything you need to change your décor as Mother Nature spins her magic.

From basic supplies and flowers to elaborate centerpieces and topiaries, everyone will find his or her niche. Flip through the pages and get a feel for what interests you. Are you looking for a modern topiary, a holiday-inspired arrangement, or a simple decoration to brighten up an otherwise drab spot in your home? Once you have an idea for the space you'd like to fill and the mood you'd like to create, dig in. Use several projects as inspiration. Choose flowers or colors from one, a container from another, or the type of display from yet another.

While the book is broken down by season, giving hints on which flowers to look for, you will also find that many arrangements stand their ground year round. If you're a fan of the English garden look, Asian-inspired décor, or wandering ivy, you'll find all in the following pages. If you just need to add an accent to a decorating scheme, try candleholders or dress up a mirror.

Silk flowers aren't just for indoors anymore. There are many wonderful displays for garden parties, cookouts, and spooky Halloween fun. You'll find ways to decorate stairs, gardens, fences, and porches. Place flowers along walkways or poolside, or decorate around a mailbox or garage. These flowers won't get dug up, and they won't need to be replanted. The best thing about dried and silk flowers is the ease with which your theme can be carried from outside to inside and from room to room.

Each chapter also contains a spattering of holiday-inspired décor. In Spring, Easter is on our minds. Summer brings the Fourth of July, Autumn decorations center around Thanksgiving and Halloween, and Christmas is the most-decorated Winter holiday. While any display can be changed with just a few new color or floral choices, the holiday-specific displays will give you a starting point to get your home ready for that festive celebration.

COLOR KEY	
	Spring
	Summer
	Autumn
	Winter
	Containers

This book is your complete resource for arranging silk and dried flowers. If you have little or no experience with flowers, start at the beginning. All the necessary supplies are pictured and identified. The sample projects show you how to use them, and the library of flowers and foliage are a wealth of inspiration.

If it's the pot that has you stuck, flip to the back of the book. The last chapter is all about containers. You will find samples of everything from terra cotta and glass to an old boot.

This is your home, fill it with flowers, and it will always be a comforting and inviting place to live!

Enjoy!

Table of Contents

Flowers have long been used to symbolize everything from true love to disappointment and rejection. While you may choose to research the meaning behind your blooms, it is more common to choose arrangements based on color, size, and appropriateness. Some flowers may not look right in your kitchen, but those same blooms could be a perfect accent in a guest room or sitting room.

This section includes basic techniques to guide you through the process of creating centerpieces, topiaries, wreaths, and swags. To complete these floral arrangements, you will need an assortment of flowers, a Dried Flower Sealant, and the supplies shown on the following pages.

Bird and butterfly picks

Decorative stones

Decorative stones

Vegetable pick

Various picks

Pinecones, dried pods, and fungi

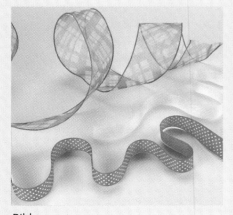
Ribbons

Leaves

Wreath hangers

Containers

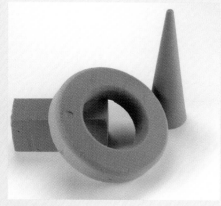
Foam shapes

Basic wreaths

Mosses

Candleholders

Floral picks and pins

Wire snips

Floral tape

Various wires

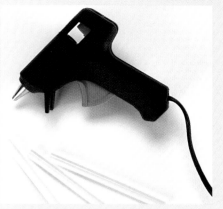
Hot glue gun and glue sticks

While it would be impossible to teach you everything about floral arrangements in a few pages, the following examples should give you enough information to start you in the right direction. Once you understand some basic terminology and design concepts, you should be able to apply them to all types of projects, including centerpieces, topiaries, wreaths, and swags.

Focal flowers are the foundation of each arrangement. These are the flowers that will draw the most attention. It is standard to use odd numbers of focal flowers in arrangements. **Line flowers** give an arrangement height and width and create a look of balance. Often, they have buds on a tall stalk, like gladiolas and delphiniums. **Mass flowers** add fullness to an arrangement. They are usually round and are often referred to as face flowers. They have one flower per stem and provide the focal point of color. Roses, sunflowers, and carnations are all examples of mass flowers. **Fillers**, which can be both flowers and leaves, provide a finishing touch and a full feeling. They are usually small, have numerous buds per stem, and give a smooth transition between mass flowers and line flowers. Some of the most common fillers are baby's breath, eucalyptus, and ferns.

There are numerous design principles to keep in mind when you are working with floral arrangements. **Balance** refers to the overall symmetry of the arrangement and how the individual parts of the design relate to one another. One way to add interest to the design is with **contrast**, both in the colors that are used and the "mix" of flowers and foliage. A design that has **rhythm** helps move the eye smoothly through it.

Use the photos on the following pages to help you choose the flowers and greens for your arrangements.

2

3

1. Place the wired floral pick against the side of the stem.
2. Wrap the wire around the stem.

3. Wrap floral tape around the pick and stem. Cut the tape about an inch from the end of the stem.

TIP

If the smaller filler flowers and leaves have limp stems, you may need to reinforce them with a wire pick.

USING FLORAL TAPE

While holding the items to be taped together in your left hand along with the start of the floral tape, hold the roll of tape with your right hand. Use tension as you pull the tape off of the roll and twist the items to "wrap" them with tape.

Carnations

Snowball

Zinnias

Peony with bud

Heleniums

Freesia spray

Tiger lilies

Lilac

Snapdragons

Gladiolas

Ranunculus spray

Rose

Rose

Sunflower

Peony

Gerbera daisy

Marigold spray

Dogwood

Celusia

Rose spray

Cycas fern

Ivy

Ivy spray

Eucalyptus

Queen Ann's Lace

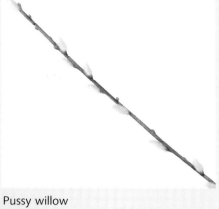

Pussy willow

Cattail with onion grass

Grass spray

Asparagus fern

Large grass spray

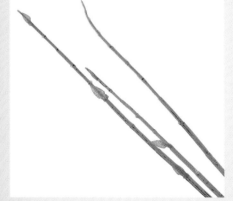

Bamboo

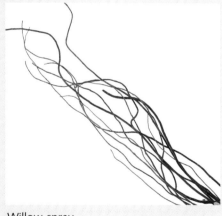

Willow spray

Grape leaves

Berry spray

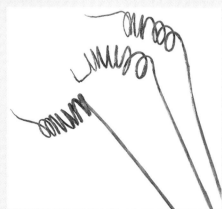

Curly willow spray

Dusty miller

2

3

CENTERPIECE

This basic centerpiece is simple to complete, yet adds a great deal of color and interest to your table. Choose focal flowers that complement your décor.

1. Cut the foam to fit the container, and press in place. The foam should be flush or slightly above the top of the container to allow for trailing foliage.

2. Using floral pins, attach the moss. Pin securely at the corners of the foam.

3. Cut the stems on the flowers to 1½". Outlining the top of the pot, stick the line flowers and foliage into the moss-covered foam. For added security, glue them in place.

4. Arrange the five focal flowers to add height to your arrangement.

5. Add the three mass flowers along the base of the arrangement. Roses were used here.

6. Add filler leaves to define the shape.

7. Add filler flowers as desired. Bend and shape your arrangement to look natural.

4

5

6

7

The completed centerpiece.

3   4   5

TOPIARY WITH FLOWERS

Topiaries are really coming into vogue for weddings and other gatherings. They make great centerpieces, and they look stylish near an entranceway or fireplace.

1. Cut the foam to fit the container, and press in place. Arrange the Spanish moss on top of the foam.
2. Stick one end of the dowel into the bottom of the foam ball, and stick the other end into the moss.
3. Cut stems to surround the dowel. Trim off the leaves, and stick the stems in the moss.

4. Use wire to secure the stems near the top of the dowel.
5. Cut all of the roses, so the stems are the same length. Stick them into the foam ball, overlapping the petals so the foam ball doesn't show.
6. Wind berry vines around the bottom of the stems.
7. Take the wire off the floral pick, and push it into the bird. Push the bird into the pot.
8. Hot glue the natural elements along the rim of the pot.

6

7

8

9

The completed topiary.

WREATH

Wreaths are common Christmas decorations, and this unique design would certainly be a welcome addition. It's also simple enough to use with any fall or winter design scheme.

1. Spray each rose bud with Dried Flower Sealant, and cut the buds off the stems.

2. Hot glue the white flowers along the twig wreath form, following the curve of the branches.

3. Hot glue the rose buds in groups of two around the inner circle of the wreath. Leave a small space for the leaves between each group of rose buds.

4. Hot glue the leaves between the rose buds.

The completed wreath

Nature in Neutrals, page 29

CHAPTER ONE

Spring

The first days of Spring are always a welcome respite from the frost and cold of winter. Flowers bloom, baby animals are born, birds are singing, and everyone's outside. Many are planning this year's garden and searching hopefully for plants that survived the winter.

It's easy to make decorations that echo this rebirth. When you're planning Spring celebrations, like Easter egg hunts, graduation parties, and bridal showers, decorate with pastels. Your patio and backyard will look great in baby pink, lavender, sunny yellow, lime green, and sky blue.

Tulips, daffodils, and irises make nice spring arrangements. If you're fortunate enough to have a lilac bush nearby, be sure to enjoy a few bouquets. These wonderfully fragrant blooms don't last long.

Floral arrangements that add to the joy of being outside are always fun. Decorate fences and porches to welcome the change of the seasons. Add decorative picks with baby birds, a frog, or even a lucky bug.

Don't forget to decorate your garden. A nice arbor or pretty plant pokes will make pulling weeds less of a dreaded task.

Other spring flowers include: roses, hyacinths, violets, calla lilies, peonies, and lilies of the valley. Use ivy and moss as filler.

English Garden

Evoke the feeling of an English garden in your home with this easy-to-make arrangement.

Designed by Kim Wakefield
Difficulty level: Intermediate

YOU WILL NEED

6½" x 12" x 8" basket without handle*
4 small English ivy bushes
3 blue/violet lace delphinium stems
3 pink sweet pea stems
1 sage/green amaranthus stem
1 pkg. white paper roses
1 green/burgundy berry spray
1 pkg. curly willow branches
36 length of ⅜" dowel
Green moss
4 foam blocks
Brown acrylic paint
Coping saw, hot glue gun and glue sticks, ruler, small
    paintbrush, wire cutters

*If the basket has a handle, use wire cutters to remove it.

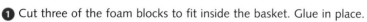

1 Cut three of the foam blocks to fit inside the basket. Glue in place.
2 Cut the dowel in half. Paint both 18" pieces brown. Glue the dowels in the foam on opposite ends. The dowels will stabilize the top part of the arrangement. Cover the foam with moss and glue in place.
3 Cut the curly willow into 16" lengths. Insert it in the foam, around the dowels.
4 Apply hot glue on the tops of the dowels. Press the remaining piece of foam over the dowels. Press down firmly until the willow ends are up against the foam.
5 Insert one English ivy bush in the foam, on the left side of the basket, with several stems draped over to the right side. Insert one ivy bush in the center of the top foam block, draping ivy over all of the sides. Cut apart the remaining bushes and randomly insert pieces into the top and bottom foam blocks to cover them completely.
6 Cut the florals and berry stems apart. Randomly arrange them amongst the ivy.

Spring Basket

Filled with a wide array of spring flowers, including tulips, irises, and daffodils, this is the perfect arrangement to display inside or out.

Designed by Kathryn Severns
Difficulty level: Easy

YOU WILL NEED

5 small irises, light purple
3 large irises, dark purple
5 tulips, white
5 daffodils, yellow
5 dogwood sprays, pink
5 forsythia sprays
7 strands of grapevine
8½" x 6" x 3½" woven basket
Dry floral foam
Hot glue gun and glue sticks, wire cutters

1 Center and glue the floral foam into the bottom of the basket.

2 Insert the white tulips, positioning the flowers toward the center of floral foam (approximately 1" from the back edge of the foam).

3 Add the daffodils and irises to the arrangement. Clip the stems as needed to maintain a consistent height.

4 Place the forsythia sprays at the back of the floral foam, one on either side of the arrangement and one in the center. Spread the branches of the spray apart to fill in empty spaces in the arrangement. Cut the two remaining forsythia sprays apart and insert into the arrangement as filler.

5 Insert the dogwood sprays as needed to fill in the arrangement.

Cup of Color

Designed by Kathryn Severns
Difficulty level: Easy

This cute cup will look right at home on a windowsill, your desk, or anyplace you need a dash of color.

YOU WILL NEED

Coffee cup
Foam ball*
1 bunch African violets
Spanish moss
Hot glue gun and glue sticks,
   scissors, wire cutters
*This ball should be the same
   width as the coffee cup.

❶ Push the ball inside the coffee cup so that the top of the ball is about ½" from the top of the cup. Glue in place.
❷ Glue Spanish moss around the edge of the foam ball. Allow moss to hang over the edge of the cup.
❸ Remove the leaves from the African violet bunch and set aside. Cut the stem of the violet bunch with wire cutters, leaving enough remaining to go through the foam ball. Push the stem through the center of the ball, and pull it back out. Fill the hole with glue and reinsert the stem.
❹ Shape the violets to form a round shape over the foam ball.
❺ Position the leaves cut in Step 3 around the edge of the cup, and glue in place.

Oriental Bouquet

With its simple lines, this elegant centerpiece can be made in about an hour.

Designed by Ritsu Waggoner
Difficulty level: Easy

YOU WILL NEED

4" x 9" cylindrical ivory vase*
2 pkg. natural dry bamboo stems*
1 pkg. natural dry bamboo with
    twisted vine stems*
2 irises with buds*
1 bamboo green stem*
2 rice flowers*
1 iris*
Green moss
Bag of raffia
1 foam brick
Hot glue gun and glue sticks, ruler,
    serrated knife, wire cutters

*Used in this project: Haeger vase;
 Tropical Splendor rice flower,
 green bamboo; Everyday Collection cherry blossom, iris.

❶ Use the serrated knife to cut the foam to fit in the vase, and glue it in place. Cover the foam with green moss, gluing on the edge only.

❷ Cut the natural dry bamboo stems to 9" lengths, and glue around the vase.

❸ Tie a few strands of raffia around the bottom of the vase.

❹ Cut three 4" bamboo stems. Tie two together with raffia, and glue to the front of the vase at an angle.

❺ Apply hot glue on the ends of the stems and insert into the foam in the vase.

❻ Place 26" and 28" bamboo with vines slightly behind the center of the vase. Insert two iris buds with leaves near the bamboo. Insert one bamboo green stem on the left.

❼ Cut one rice flower stem to 20", and cut the remaining stem very short. Insert on the right side of the arrangement.

❽ Insert the cherry blossom on the left and the iris flower in the center.

Flower Bulbs

Designed by Kristy McNeil
Difficulty level: Advanced

Here you will be creating a bulb with foam!

YOU WILL NEED

Foam egg*
Syndicate Sales Everlasting Elegance™ artificial water*
Vase with narrow opening**
Burnt sienna and burnt umber acrylic paints*
Krylon™ Frosted Glass™ paint (optional)
Tacky glue*
3 pieces 6" x 7" crinkled crepe paper, tan
1 artificial orchid plant with roots
River rocks
Disposable plastic container and spoon, funnel, masking tape (optional), paintbrush (#12 Flat), scissors, serrated knife, wire cutters

*Used in this project: Syndicate Sales Plastifoam™ Duck Egg; Plaid Enterprises Folk Art™ Artist Acrylics; Aleene's Tacky Glue™.
**You may use any vase where the egg fits snugly in the opening.

❶ Shape the foam egg into a teardrop. Use the serrated knife to shave the egg toward the pointed end. Cut out irregular chunks. Squeeze the foam until the desired shape is achieved.
❷ Cut the orchid stem from the roots with wire cutters. Insert the orchid stem through the narrow end of the egg to create a starter hole for later. Remove the stem. Repeat on the larger end of the egg.
❸ Cut the crepe paper into strips. You will need approximately ten of each size: ½" x 4" and ½" x 2". Fold each strip in half.
❹ To create the bulb's texture, apply tacky glue with the paintbrush on the egg and add a 4" paper strip, starting at the pointed end of the egg. The unfolded ends should be pointed up. Open the folded strip part and apply more glue with the flat paintbrush. Paint on more glue to secure. Repeat this process with the 4" strips to completely cover the egg. Overlap the strips slightly. Allow the paper to become wrinkled and wooden looking. **Note:** Layering and wrinkling the paper is important for an authentic look.
❺ Use the smaller pieces of crepe paper around the narrow end, around the hole. Allow the glued pieces to dry.
❻ Where a strip covers one of the holes in the top or bottom of the egg, re-insert the orchid stem to keep the paper from clogging the holes.
❼ Using the flat brush, apply burnt sienna paint, starting from the wider end. Apply more pressure on the brush toward the wider end of the egg, lightening up to a dry brush toward the top. Let dry.
❽ Apply burnt umber paint to the wider portion of the egg. Stop the color about halfway up the egg. Let dry.

❾ Dip the orchid stem into the glue. Insert the stem in the narrow end of the bulb. For a tight hold, stop pushing when the foam resists.
❿ Clip the roots from the large taped stem. Dip into glue and insert into the bottom of the egg.
⓫ Wash and thoroughly dry the vase and the river rock.
⓬ With masking tape, mask a line around the vase where the frost will end to protect the top half of the glass from over spray. Apply the Frosted Glass paint. Allow to dry before touching.
⓭ Place the river rocks in the vase.
⓮ In the disposable container, mix the contents of the Everlasting Elegance package. Mix for at least three minutes to combine properly. Scrape the sides of the container while mixing.
⓯ Place the funnel in the vase opening. Pour the mixture into the vase. Pour any remaining mixture back in the original bottle and allow to cure (or use the extra for another project immediately).
⓰ Place the flower and bulb assembly in the vase opening. It should fit snugly. Allow the assembly to remain undisturbed for 24 to 48 hours.

Everlasting Plantings

These unique arrangements can be made in virtually no time at all!

Designed by Kristy McNeil
Difficulty level: Easy

YOU WILL NEED

Syndicate Sales Everlasting Elegance™
   artificial water
Clear glass vase*
Artificial flowering plants with foliage
   and roots attached (amaryllis and
   orchids are shown)
River rocks
Disposable plastic container and spoon,
   funnel, masking tape

*Used in this project: Syndicate Sales
#4114 cut-off vase and footed vase.

❶ Wash and thoroughly dry the vase and river rocks. Add about three quarters of the river rocks to the vase.
❷ In the disposable container, mix the contents of the Everlasting Elegance package. Mix for at least three minutes to combine properly. Scrape the sides of the container while mixing. Add the mixture to the vase.
❸ Create a tape grid on the vase, over the opening, leaving a hole in the center. Place the plant through the grid, in the center of the mixture. Push gently to bring rocks around the base of the plant. If necessary, further secure the plant with additional tape.
❹ Allow the arrangement to remain undisturbed for 24 to 48 hours.

Breath of Spring

Graceful ivy and pastel-colored flowers adorn this pretty cone.

Designed by Edwin R. Smith
Difficulty level: Intermediate

YOU WILL NEED

12" x 5" STYROFOAM® brand foam cone
1" STYROFOAM® brand foam ball
36 silk pansies, multiple colors
5 tulips, lavender
6 daffodils, yellow
3 lupine, blue
Ivy, variegated
24 large leaves
3 yds. 1¾" wide sheer ribbon, lavender
Chenille stem
Latex gloves, low-temp glue gun and glue sticks or thick white craft glue, newspapers, scissors, 6" wooden skewer, spray adhesive, 3" wooden picks, wire cutters

❶ Press the foam cone against a tabletop to flatten one side so it will hang flat against a wall. Insert the skewer into the cone's tip.

❷ Remove the plastic veins from the large silk leaves, and discard them. Place the leaves front side down on the newspaper. Wearing latex gloves, spray the leaves and cone with adhesive. When the adhesive is tacky to the touch, smooth the leaves on the cone, overlapping them slightly.

❸ Twist the chenille stem into a loop and insert into the flat topside of the cone as a hanger. Secure with glue.

❹ Push the foam ball onto the tip of cone, gluing it in place. Glue the pansy blossoms on the ball, covering it completely.

❺ Gently shape the flower stems for a natural appearance. Add the wooden picks to the flowers for added length, if needed. Dip the flower stems into glue before inserting them into the cone.

❻ With wire cutters, cut the lupine stems into lengths of 8", 10", and 15". Insert a 15" stem of lupine into the top left of the cone. Insert the 8" stem in the middle and the 10" stem trailing over the left side.

❼ Cut one tulip stem to 12", one 10", and three 8". Insert the 12" stem to right of the tallest lupine. Insert the 10" tulip trailing down the right side of the cone. Insert the 8" stems, filling in the center of the design.

❽ Cut the stem of one daffodil to 8", two 6", and three 4". Insert the 8" daffodil below the tallest tulip. Insert the remaining daffodils in the center of the design, as pictured.

❾ Add pansies and ivy around the flowers. Glue one strand of ivy trailing down the front of the cone. Glue pansies to the trailing ivy.

❿ Cut the ribbon into 1-yard lengths. Attach wooden picks to the ends of two of the lengths. Insert the ribbon into the cone around the flowers as graceful loops. Glue the last length of ribbon trailing out the right side. Trim the ends of ribbon into a "V" shape.

Nature in Neutrals

Neutral colors are so peaceful and relaxing, and this arrangement of "antiqued" flowers is quite stunning. Add a few stems of silk flowers in colors that complement the antiqued, and your arrangement will take on a naturalized, "realistic" look, giving the appearance that while some flowers are aging, new life is springing forth.

Designed by Lisa Galvin
Difficulty level: Easy

YOU WILL NEED

6½" plastic container, peach*
3" x 4" x 8" piece of floral foam*
1 stem antique hydrangea, sage
3 stems antique delphinium
1 stem antique rose buds x 6, lavender
2 stems magnolia x 3, peach tones
1 stem magnolia x 3, pale fern green
1 stem tiger lily x 3 w/buds, lavender
Kiwi vine, natural
Spanish moss
Ming moss
Glue gun and glue sticks, knife, ruler, wire cutters

*Used in this project: Syndicate Sales Jardiniere Plastic Container, #34 and Floralfoam^{SM} Brick.

Tip
Stuff recycled plastic grocery bags inside of the container, around the floral foam, to keep it firmly in place. This prevents any wobbling that might dislodge its hold on the bottom of the container when the arrangement is added. It serves a wonderful purpose and saves you the expense of additional filler!

❶ Cut the floral foam with the knife so that the top is about level with the top of the container. Glue the foam to the bottom of the container, and cover the top with Spanish moss to conceal it from view.

❷ **Note:** Although primarily viewed from the front, flowers should be inserted around all sides of the container for best results. Begin by establishing key elements of the design: the kiwi vine, delphiniums, and hydrangea. Divide one delphinium stem into two separate stems, by cutting it approximately 9" down the stem with wire cutters, near the emerging flowers on the lower stem section. Leave a tiny stub of stem wire exposed and create a second stem to add to the arrangement later. The flowers remaining on the bottom portion of the original stem easily conceal the wire stub. Beginning near the center, insert all of the delphinium stems into the foam, referring to photo for placement. Next add the hydrangea and kiwi vine.

❸ Fill in any spaces with the remaining flowers.

❹ Randomly glue Ming moss around the edges.

Stucco Arbor

Designed by Kristy McNeil
Difficultly level: Advanced

Can you believe this beautiful arbor is made from foam? With various pieces of foam and everyday tools and supplies you, too, can create a masterpiece!

YOU WILL NEED

Foam: 2 sheets ½" x 12" x 36"; 1 block 2" x 12" x 18"; 2 balls 1"*
4 large and 8 small foam dragonflies*
Hot craft knife with blade tip*
Acrylic paint, green
Sweet pea garland
Lavender bush
1 package reindeer moss
Sheet moss
4 double-ended chair rail outside corners, 5¾" tall
1 qt. latex paint, soft green
Fume mask, greening pins, hammer, liquid nails (for heavy-duty construction), matte knife, 1" bristle brush, ⅛" dowel, paper, pencil, sand texture (additive for paint), scissors, short pins (10mm), toothpicks, yard stick
*Used in this project: Syndicate Sales Plastifoam foam; Design-A-Line™ Kreative Foam™; Dremel Versatip™; Plaid Enterprises Folk Art Artists Acrylics, Olive Green; McCloskey's Cactus Green latex paint.

Foam Cutting Tips
- While cutting the foam, wear a mask. The fumes from melting craft foam can be irritating.
- To make cutting easier, place the foam above the worktable by sitting the edges on top of extra foam blocks or books. Place the area that will be cut between these items. Glide the blade completely through the foam. If you need to stop, pull up in a smooth motion. If the blade gets caught up, pull up then wipe it on an old piece of wood. Allow the excess foam to burn off. Continue cutting.

1. Insert the blade tip and plug in the knife.
2. Enlarge the arbor pattern to an 18" height. Cut out and pin the pattern onto one of the ½" foam sheets.
3. Use the hot knife to cut the pattern from the foam. Cut out the wings, and flatten slightly with the hammer.
4. Cut out the following pieces from ½" foam: 5" x 16" (three), 5" x 6" (two), 3" x 16¼" (two), 3" x 5¼" (two).
5. Apply glue to the end of one of the 5" x 16" pieces. Press onto one of the 5" x 6" pieces to form one corner of the box. Break the toothpicks in half and insert to secure the joints. Apply glue to the bottom inside edge of the two pieces. Attach one of the 5" x 16" pieces to form the box bottom, and secure with toothpicks. Attach the last 5" x 16" piece to form the other long side of the box. Secure with toothpicks and glue. Attach the last 5" x 6" piece with glue, and secure with toothpicks.
6. Mount the wooden corner pieces so that the bottom end acts as a foot for the box and the top creates a finial.
7. Gently tap the longest edges of the remaining cut pieces with the hammer to bevel. Glue the pieces to the box as pictured. Secure with cut toothpicks.
8. For the sides, use one smaller dragonfly in the center. Add the remaining dragonflies.
9. Following the manufacturer's directions, add sand texture to the latex paint until the sand particles are clearly visible. Mix thoroughly.
10. Apply one coat of the sandy paint to the entire box. Apply to the inside about one quarter of the way down. Set aside to dry.
11. Glue the balls to the ends of the arbor and secure with toothpicks. Paint the arbor as in Step 10. Let dry.
12. Apply another coat of sand paint to all of the pieces. If the foam still shows, add another coat and let dry.
13. Cut two 4½" x 15½" pieces from the 2" thick block. Glue one piece to the bottom of the box. Glue the second to the first.
14. Cut the dowel into four 4" pieces. Glue and insert the dowel pieces into the bottom of the arbor.
15. Glue and insert the arbor into the box, one-quarter of the way from the back of the block.
16. Use greening pins to add a layer of sheet moss to the box. Insert the lavender bush on the right side. Be careful not to push too hard on the bottom of the box. Make a starter hole, if necessary.
17. Cut the garland in half. Insert it into the left side of the box and weave through the arbor. Insert the remaining pieces of garland in the back and down in the front.
18. For added color, pin reindeer moss wherever the sheet moss shows.

Topiary Trio

Designed by Kristy McNeil
Difficulty level: Advanced

YOU WILL NEED

For Bee
Foam: egg, 1½" ball, ½" thick piece (3" x 8")*
1 oz. each poppy seeds, orange peel, and
   spearmint

For Butterfly
Foam: 1" ball (2), 1½" ball, 1" x 3" disk, 1" x 4"
   disk, ½" thick piece (3" x 12")*
¼" dowel
1 oz. dulce, poppy seeds, orange peel, spearmint

For Dragonfly
Foam: duck egg, 1½" ball, 1" ball (4), ½" thick
   piece (4" x 8")*
¼" dowel
1 oz. lavender flowers, poppy seeds, passion
   flower, spearmint

For All
Tacky glue*
Acrylic paint, red green and white*
Crackle medium*
Spray paint, flat black*
Unfinished wood candlestick
1 stem artificial aster flowers
Floral clay, fume mask, hammer, hot craft knife
   with blade tip*, hot glue gun and glue sticks,
   1" sponge paintbrush, paper plates, pins
   (10mm) scissors, thick armature wire, tooth-
   picks, wire cutters

*Used in this project: Syndicate Sales Plastifoam;
Aleene's Tacky Glue; Plaid Enterprises Folk Art
Artist Acrylics, Clover and Titanium White and
Crackle Medium; Krylon™ Spray Enamel; Dremel
Versatip™.

Covered with such fragrant items as lavender and orange peel, this thre looks—and smells—delightful.

For All

1 Spray the wire with black paint. Set aside.

2 Apply a mixture of two parts green paint and one part white to the candlestick. Let dry. Apply a coat of crackle medium, following the manufacturer's directions. Let dry.

3 Fill the candlestick opening with floral clay. Cut flowers from the stems and insert into the clay. If desired, use leaves to hide the floral clay.

4 Bevel the edges of each foam disk by pushing the edges onto the worktable. Attach the 3" disk on top of the 4" disk with a toothpick and glue.

5 Apply glue to the joined disks and cover with spearmint.

6 Hot-glue the 3" disk to the bottom of the candlestick.

Bee

1 Insert the blade tip and plug in the knife.

2 Make two copies of the wing pattern on page 35, and cut them out.

3 Pin the patterns to the ½" thick piece of foam. Cut out the wings with the hot knife. Flatten the edges and top with the hammer.

4 Apply tacky glue to one side of each wing piece. Pour the spearmint on a plate and press the pieces into the spearmint. Continue applying glue to the wing and adhering spearmint until both wings are entirely covered. Set aside to dry.

5 Apply glue to the 1½" foam ball, and roll it in the poppy seeds, completely covering it. Set aside to dry.

6 Apply two bands of glue around the egg, one on one end and another about ¾" from it. Gently roll the egg in the poppy seeds. Let dry. Now apply glue to the uncovered sections of the egg. Press the orange peel into the glued areas. Let dry.

7 Use tacky glue and toothpicks to secure the ball to the wider end of the egg. Add the wings.

8 Coil the armature wire as desired. Dip the wire in tacky glue, and insert into the center of the body.

9 Insert the wire into the floral clay in the candlestick.

Butterfly

1 Insert the blade tip and plug in the knife.

2 Make two copies of the wing pattern on page 35, and cut them out.

3 Pin the wings to the ½" thick piece of foam. Cut out the wings with the hot knife. Flatten slightly with the hammer.

4 Following the pattern, use tacky glue to outline the details on the front and back of each wing. Pour the poppy seeds on a plate, and sprinkle the glued areas with the seeds. Very lightly press the glued areas to set. Tap to remove excess.

5 Slice about one quarter of the 1½" ball on each side. Push the edges with your fingers to form an oblong body.

6 Dip a toothpick in glue, and insert ¾" into one end of the body. Apply more glue to the toothpick, and insert it into one of the 1" balls. Insert another toothpick into the other end of the body.

7 Cut the other 1" ball in half, and roll it in your hands. Attach it to the toothpick.

8 Apply glue to the body and cover with dulce. Tap to remove the excess. Add dulce to the upper portion of the wings. Let dry. Add Orange Peel to the lower portion of the wings. Let dry.

9 Cut the dowel to the height you desire, and paint it black. Let dry.

10 Insert one end of the dowel into the bottom of the butterfly's body, and insert the other end into the candlestick.

Dragonfly

1 Insert the blade tip and plug in the knife.

2 Make four copies of the wing pattern on page 35, and cut them out. Pin wing patterns to the ½" thick piece of foam. Cut out the wings with the hot knife. Flatten the edges and top with the hammer.

3 Apply tacky glue to one side of each wing piece. Pour the lavender on a plate. Press the piece into the lavender. Continue covering the wing with glue and lavender. Let dry. Repeat for the three remaining wings.

4 Cover the 1½" ball, egg, and two of the 1" balls with poppy seeds. Let dry. Cover the two remaining 1" balls with passion flower.

5 Cut the dowel to the height you desire, and paint it black. Let dry.

6 Use tacky glue and toothpicks to secure the larger ball to the wider end of the egg. Secure the balls to the smaller end of the egg and to each other. Add the wings.

7 Insert one end of the dowel into the bottom of the butterfly's body, and insert the other end into the candlestick.

Arbor Pattern.
Photocopy at 200%.

Chair Back Swag, page 41

CHAPTER TWO

Summer

Summer is the season where everyone gets to be a kid again. Although you may not get to sleep until noon and spend the rest of the day lounging on the beach, there are many causes for celebration and decoration!

Bright colors make clear that it's time to celebrate. Use primary colors to decorate for family reunions and Fourth of July celebrations. Make your bouquets with daisies, gardenias, and ranunculus.

Fresh fruits and vegetable are in great abundance during the summer months. Picking strawberries and rounding up the perfect watermelon are common traditions. Why not carry those themes into your décor? Use strawberry picks or a watermelon theme to give your kitchen or bathroom a pick-me-up.

And, don't forget about picnics! Whether you're out on a blanket in a meadow with your sweetie or "picnicking" around the pool with 100 of your closest friends, flowers will give your day a touch of elegance that your guests won't soon forget.

Other summer flowers include: roses, delphiniums, tulips, peonies, and big gerbera daisies. Use herbs and ivy as filler.

IN THIS CHAPTER

Vegetable Topiary

Summer's bounty is given center stage in this unique arrangement that incorporates wire mesh.

Designed by Edwin R. Smith
Difficulty level: Intermediate

YOU WILL NEED

16" x 20" sheet of ½" aluminum mesh
9" tall x 6" wide galvanized flower bucket
1 large carrot
2 medium carrots
4 small carrots
2 tomatoes
1 red pepper
Assorted small vegetables
Maiden hair fern
Small sunflowers
Small green blossoms
3 heavy stems or sticks, each 18" long
12" x 6" x 2" foam sheet
Green sheet moss
2 cups gravel
Floral wire (24 gauge), floral U pins, gloves, hot glue gun and glue sticks, knife, ruler, wire cutters

*Used in this project: WireForm® Gallery Mesh American Art Clay; STYROFOAM® brand foam.

❶ Place the gravel in the bucket. This will weigh the design down and prevent it from tipping.

❷ Cut the foam to fit inside the bucket so that it is level with the opening. Glue it in place. Cover the foam with sheet moss, pinning it to the foam with floral U pins.

❸ Insert and glue the heavy stems into the center of the bucket. About 15" should be visible above the bucket. Glue the tomatoes beside the stems.

❹ Wearing gloves to protect your hands, shape the wire mesh into a cone shape that will sit on top of the bucket. Trim any excess with wire cutters. The cone should be about 16" tall. Secure the cone with short lengths of floral wire.

❺ Place the cone on top of the bucket. Adjust the stems as needed to be centered inside of the cone. Insert floral U pins through the cone and into the foam. Glue the cone in place.

❻ Pin and glue a cluster of carrots to the front of the bucket at the base of the cone. Use lengths of floral wire, if needed, to secure the vegetables to the cone. Glue a small cluster of fern and vegetables near the tip of the cone. Glue the small sunflowers to the tip of the cone.

❺ Glue and wire the other vegetables and greens around the base of the cone. Cover any glue or floral U pins with bits of moss or fern.

Festive Wreath Centerpiece

This poolside centerpiece may look difficult, but it is made of pre-made floral swags, so it goes together in minutes.

Designed by Kim Wakefield
Difficulty level: Easy

YOU WILL NEED

12" green plastic foam wreath
10" green plastic saucer
12" clear cylinder candle vase
8" pillar candle
2 artificial floral swags
1 artificial English ivy garland
Plastic fruit: 7 lemon halves, 4 apple halves, 1 medium orange, 1 pomegranate
Greening pins
Wire cutters

❶ Glue the plastic saucer inside the center of the foam wreath.
❷ Unwind the ivy garland, and wrap it around the middle outer edge of the wreath. Hold it in place with greening pins. Cut off any excess ivy.
❸ Shape the swags to fit the curve of the wreath. Place over the ivy and work the ivy in with the swags. Hold in place with greening pins.
❹ Randomly glue fruits on the wreath. Glue the glass candle cylinder in the center of the saucer. Place the candle inside the cylinder.

Chair Back Swag

Designed by Elaine Schmidt
Difficulty level: Intermediate

YOU WILL NEED

2 rose hip berry sprays
6 long ivy garlands
4 small wild rose sprays
9 yds. 1½" sheer wire-edge ribbon, pink
5 yds. 1½" wire-edge ribbon, floral
Chair
Floral wire, hot glue gun and glue sticks

This swag is a perfect accent for the guest of honor's chair at a special summer occasion.

1 To form the base of the swag, overlap the ends of the sprays and temporarily wire them together. Curve the sprays into a "U" shape that fits on the back of the chair. Make any necessary adjustments and wire permanently in several places to hold the sprays together.

2 Cut the garland in half and wire each piece onto the swag.

3 Cut two 2½-yard lengths of pink ribbon. Make a knot to hold the ribbons together about 18" from one end. Place this knot at one end of the swag and tie the streamers to the back of the swag. These streamers will be used to tie the swag onto the chair.

4 Loop the long lengths of ribbon through the swag. When you reach the other side of the swag, knot the two ribbon ends together and attach by knotting the streamers at the back. These streamers will be used to tie the swag onto the chair.

5 Position and glue the wild rose sprays onto the swag.

6 Cut two 2½-yard lengths of floral ribbon. Form each length into a six-loop bow with long streamers. Cut the remaining pink ribbon in half. Form each length into a slightly smaller six-loop bow with long streamers. Wire the pink bows to the center of the floral bows.

7 Wire and glue the completed bows to each side of the swag at the point where the sheer ribbon streamers are knotted onto the swag.

8 Trim all of the ribbon streamers on an angle or a "V" shape.

9 To attach the swag to the chair, tie the sheer ribbon streamers around the top of the chair and let them hang behind the swag.

Hot Tropics Swag

Designed by Gail Gregor
Difficulty level: Intermediate

The bright colors of the tropics are an interesting mate to an ordinary tree branch!

YOU WILL NEED

42" long forked tree branch, completely dry
5 stems of Boston fern*
2 artificial hedge apples
2 stems of permanent botanical (silk) lime green orchids*
2 stems of orchids, hot pink*
2 stems of anthuriums, lime green*
2 stems of pincushion proteas, lime green*
4 stems of peony buds, hot pink*
4 stems of statice, hot pink*
2 stems of "tilandsia plant"*
8 stems of lily grass, variegated*
2 pieces of Spanish moss*
1 foam disk, 2" x 4"*
1 sheet of decorator moss
6 greening pins
Brown floral tape, floral wire (18 gauge or 20 gauge),
     hot glue gun and glue sticks, wire cutters

*Used in this project: STYROFOAM brand foam; perma-
nent botanical.

Tip
If needed, use floral picks to insert the flowers and
foliage into the foam at the base of the design.

❶ Evaluate the branch, and choose the best side and angle. If necessary, use wire cutters to prune any excess branches or twigs.

❷ To cover the wire with the brown floral tape, start at one end and carefully spiral the tape downward until the entire wire is covered. Cover 10 pieces of wire.

❸ Cover all sides of the foam disk with the sheet moss. Use as few greening pins as possible to secure the moss to the foam. Do not glue the moss to the foam.

❹ Place the moss-covered foam disk in the center of the branch. Use the brown covered wire to secure the disk to the branch. Make sure the disk won't move.

❺ When adding the flowers, work from the center outward. Begin with the hedge apples to create focal emphasis. Make a hole in each apple, wide enough to insert the end of a stem. Insert a piece of stem approximately 2" long into each apple, and glue it into the hole. With one apple, insert the other end of the stem into the foam disk, toward the lower left. Use the glue gun to secure. Repeat for the second apple, but place it in the upper right area.

❻ Use wire cutters to cut the stems of the pincushion proteas to about 3" to 4" long. Refer to the photo for placement, and use the glue gun to secure them in place.

❼ Cut one green anthurium to 12" long, and cut the other one to 15" long. Place the shorter one in the upper right area. Place the longer one directly below it, facing slightly forward from the back. Glue all stems in place with the glue gun after they are in the proper position. Bend and shape each stem before and after placement.

❽ Cut the two stems of green orchids to 15" to 20" long, depending on the size of the branch. Position the green orchid stems in the upper left region of the design, try to follow the curve of a branch if possible. If the stems will not stay in posi-

tion, use a small piece of the brown covered wire to secure them to the branch. Stems such as the orchids should be manipulated open and all should be given slight bends to make them look real.

❾ Cut the hot pink orchids to 15" to 20" long, depending on your branch. Position the hot pink orchids on the right side of the arrangement toward the back of the branch, somewhat under the anthuriums. Wire them in place if necessary.

❿ Cut the two tilandsia plants' stems to 1" to 2" long. Position them toward the center of the foam disk, one in the upper left area and one in the lower right. Use these to fill in the design and cover the moss on the disk.

⓫ Place the four hot pink peony buds in a diagonal line from the upper left, through the center of the arrangement, and continuing on to the lower right. Adjust their stem length as necessary.

⓬ Using the picture as a guide, place the five stems of Boston fern toward the back of the branch. They should act as a filler material and as a background for the other more prominent materials.

⓭ The pink statice is a filler flower and should be used in small amounts. Place some in between the hedge apples and the proteas. Add other stems as needed to fill in and cover any remaining moss.

⓮ Add the lily grass two pieces at a time. Start in the upper left corner and use wire to secure them to a branch. The lily grass should look like a flowing ribbon on a diagonal line through the design.

⓯ Use the glue gun to attach small wisps of Spanish moss to a few of the undecorated branch sections. To complete the design, use the moss or a small leaf to cover any glue or wire that is still showing.

Ant Picnic Wreath

These fun foam ants won't ruin your picnic!

Designed by Edwin R. Smith
Difficulty level: Intermediate

YOU WILL NEED

14" straw wreath
Foam balls 3", 2", 1½", 2 each
5" diameter wicker basket
6 strawberries
1 raspberry stem
3 small mushrooms
Bear grass
Assorted foliages
Wax flower, white
2½ yds. 1½" wide ribbon, red plaid
12" bump chenille, black
Acrylic paint, black
Sheet moss, green
Floral U pins, floral wire (24 gauge), hot glue gun and sticks or heavy
   white craft glue, 1" foam brush, pearl head pins, ruler, scissors, wire
   cutters, wood floral picks

*Used in this project: STYROFOAM brand foam

① Using the foam brush, paint each of the foam balls with two coats of black, allowing the paint to dry completely between coats.

② Place the basket in the center of the wreath. Insert picks through the inside of the basket and into the wreath to hold it in place; further secure with glue. Fill the basket with sheet moss.

③ To form an ant, insert a small section of a pick into one end of a 3" ball. Insert the other end of the pick into a 2½" ball, followed by a 1½" ball. Secure with glue. Repeat for the second ant. For the legs and antenna, cut small sections of bump chenille and insert into each ant. Cut the pearl-head pins to about ½" and dip in glue. Insert in the ants for eyes.

④ Form the ribbon into a five-loop bow with loops of about 4" and streamers of 16". Secure with floral wire. Attach the bow to the upper left of the wreath with floral U pins and glue. Cascade streamers down the sides of the wreath, gluing them in place.

⑤ Insert picks into each ant and place one ant in the basket and the other ant to the left of the basket. Glue in place. Form a cluster of bear grass. Attach the cluster to a pick. Insert and glue it to the left side of the wreath, slightly behind the basket.

⑥ Cut a small section from the raspberry stem. Insert and glue the larger raspberry in the bear grass cluster. Insert and glue a small raspberry section to the bottom right of the basket. Glue the assorted foliages around the basket and ants. Glue three strawberries inside the basket. Glue the remaining strawberries as shown in the photo. Glue the mushrooms and wax flower as desired. Glue small bits of foliage to hide any glue or wires. Adjust foliages and berries as needed to create realistic lines.

⑦ Form a short length of chenille into a loop and insert it into the top back of the wreath as a hanger. Secure the loop with floral U pins and glue.

Insert wood picks into the foam to use as a handle while painting.

Patriotic Centerpiece

Designed by Sherry Bartman
Difficulty level: Easy

Show your patriotism with this grand centerpiece. Fill in the design with flags and sparkly party favors that resemble fireworks.

1 Put the bandanna in the bottom of the basket. Bring the edges over the sides of the basket. Set the floral foam into the basket, on the bandanna.

2 **Note:** As you design this arrangement, start with the tallest elements and work downward. Cut the stems of the flowers as needed to make a smooth transition from tall to short. Insert the three hyacinths into the foam, near the center.

3 Insert the red and white roses and blue and multi-colored carnations into the foam, half of each side of the handle. Mix and match the flowers as you work.

4 Insert the two large flags into the foam, pointing outward. Add the five small flags equally around the arrangement.

5 Start inserting the stars, party favors, and glittered wires into the arrangement, starting at the top and working toward the bottom.

YOU WILL NEED

14" tall (handle) x 12" diameter x 5½" high wire basket with wood handles
Large flag-designed bandanna
2 large and 5 small flags
8 roses, white
8 roses, red
8 carnations, blue
8 carnations, red, white, and blue
3 hyacinths, white
10 glitter star plant pokes, red, white, and blue
4 party favors, red, white, and blue
10 glittered wires, silver
Floral foam

Lemon Candle Centerpiece

This lemon-fresh design has a summery feeling
that will enhance your dining space.

Designed by Edwin R. Smith
Difficulty level: Intermediate

YOU WILL NEED

Glass cylinder, 9" tall x 3" wide
2 glass cylinders, 5" tall x 3" wide
12" diameter plastic tray
6 large lemons
5 medium lemons
7 small lemons
7 tiny lemons
Maiden hair fern
Green berry sprays
6 Queen Ann's lace, white
3 pillar candles, 6" tall x 3" wide, green
4 yds. 1" wide sheer ribbon, yellow
Floral wire (24 gauge), heavy white glue or low-temp
  glue gun and glue sticks, ruler, scissors, wire cutters

1 Fill each glass cylinder with lemons of different sizes. Turn the filled cylinders upside down and place in the center of the tray. Secure the cylinders to the tray with glue.

2 Glue clusters of maiden hair fern around the cylinders, extending the fern over the edges of the tray. Glue lemons of different sizes around the cylinders on top of the fern.

3 Glue the berries around the lemons. Shape the berry sprays into gentle downward curves to create a more realistic look. Cut Queen Ann's lace to short stem lengths, and glue into the design as desired.

4 Cut three 14" lengths of ribbon. Tie one length around the middle of each candle. Glue a cluster of fern and berries at the knot. Cut the remaining ribbon into 18" lengths and form into loops. Secure with floral wire. Glue the ribbon loops into the design, allowing some ribbons to cascade over the edge of the tray.

5 Place one candle on top of each lemon-filled cylinder.

Caution!
Always use caution when burning candles! Never leave burning candles unattended. Remove the ribbon from the candles as the candles burn down.

Birdhouse Wreath

Designed by Kathryn Severns
Difficulty level: Easy

Little painted birdhouses and pansies make this cheery wreath one you'll love displaying inside or out.

YOU WILL NEED

5 mini wooden birdhouses
Acrylic paint, pink, purple, magenta, lavender, yellow
Paintbrushes
Pansy blossoms: 8 purple, 5 large yellow, 7 small yellow, 7 large pink**
20" grapevine wreath
Spanish moss
Hot glue gun and glue sticks, scissors

*Used in this project: Apple Barrel Valentine Pink (20767) acrylic paint; Folk Art Purple (411) and Magenta (412) acrylic paint; DecoArt Lavender (DA34) acrylic paint; Ceramcoat Bright Yellow acrylic paint.

**You could also use a pansy garland for this project.

1 Paint the birdhouses, as shown, alternating the roof and house colors. Add painted decorations with contrasting colors. Let dry.

2 Glue Spanish moss onto the grapevine wreath, leaving vines exposed at the 12, 2, 5, 7, and 10 o'clock positions on the wreath. The birdhouses will be glued onto those spots.

3 Glue the birdhouses into the positions left in Step 2.

4 Glue the pansy blossoms onto moss, between birdhouses.

Cheerful Nosegays

Designed by Kristy McNeil
Difficulty level: Easy

YOU WILL NEED

Syndicate Sales Wonder Water™ artificial gel water
Small clear glass vase with approx. 3" opening*
Decoupage medium
6 orange or purple ranunculus (each about 2" diameter)
1 clear rubber band
Oven mitt, paper towels, saucepan (for crafts) with water, stovetop, tongs

*Used in this project: Syndicate Sales vase #4010; Plaid Enterprises Modge Podge™.

Bright orange and purple ranunculus are the perfect flowers for these simply elegant centerpieces.

Wonder Water™ is a non-permanent and re-useable flower arranging gel. If you get tired of the arrangement, just remove the stems, place the vase in warm water for 20 minutes, and pour it out. Wonder Water is also great for crafts! **Note:** You may not use a microwave to heat Wonder Water.

❶ Gather the flowers in one hand. Bring the flower heads together to make a compact circle of flowers. Place the clear rubber band around the stems up as far up as it will go.

❷ Dip the stems in decoupage medium, about 1½" up the stem. Scrape any excess medium on a paper towel. Allow the stems to dry completely before placing in the Wonder Water™. **Note:** This helps seal the stems to keep dyes from bleeding into the Wonder Water™.

❸ Place the unopened bottle of Wonder Water™ in the saucepan. Run water over the bottle until it floats. Heat the water and bottle until just under boiling temperature, then reduce heat slightly. Allow the bottle to remain in the hot water for approximately 20 minutes or until the contents are liquefied. Using the tongs and oven mitt, remove the bottle from the water. Dry off the bottle completely. If water comes in contact with the Wonder Water, it will become cloudy.

❹ Pour the Wonder Water into the vase, about one-third of the way up. If the entire bottle is not used, just replace the cap and allow to gel up again. It is re-useable!

❺ Place the stems in the Wonder Water. Let sit at room temperature. The mixture

Natural Elegance Arrangement, page 61

CHAPTER THREE

Autumn

Autumn themes are almost as abundant as the harvest. The leaves are changing, offering a variety of hues to choose from. Fields are being emptied of pumpkins, squash, and various grains.

As the temperatures are cooling, arrangements should reflect a sense of warmth. Line your walkways and stairs to welcome your guests with arrangements of sunflowers, hydrangeas, and asters. Once inside, coordinate baskets and centerpieces in yellows, oranges, deep purples, and burgundy.

If you enjoy celebrating Halloween, black cats and witches are easily incorporated into floral arrangements. Make a wooden kitty with a pumpkin for a tummy and put her out on your porch to keep the spooks away. Use a witch's hat as a centerpiece, and surround it with flowers and leaves. Vines make a festive statement weaving up to a sign or mailbox. Thanksgiving also offers a cornucopia of decorating potential. Whether you lean toward golden goblets and crystal serving dishes or paper turkeys that were traced around a child's hand, the effect is always celebratory.

Other autumn flowers include: dahlias, black-eyed susans, and chrysanthemums. Use stalks of wheat and vines full of leaves as filler.

IN THIS CHAPTER

Mushroom Cone Arrangement

The unusual shape of this wall hanging creates an interesting contrast for a narrow wall or an empty corner. The natural elegance of dried materials and feathers blend together to create a warm atmosphere with an unexpected and dramatic impact.

Designed by Diane D. Flowers
Difficulty level: Intermediate

YOU WILL NEED

5" x 18" foam cone*
6 dried mushroom pieces on wooden stems
5 dried natural or green okra pieces
5 dried poppy pods
Light and dark green reindeer moss
10 pheasant feathers
6–7 natural 8" stick pieces
Craft glue or low-temperature hot glue gun and glue
   sticks, serrated knife, wire, wire cutters, wire hooks

*Used in this project: STYROFOAM brand foam.

1. Using the knife, trim one side of the cone flat, starting at the widest point and continuing down the side for 10" to 12". This will allow the arrangement to hang more securely against the wall.

2. Cover the front, back, and base of the cone with reindeer moss, using craft glue or the glue gun.

3. To form the back of the arrangement, insert three of the dried mushroom pieces into the flat side of the base of the moss-covered cone. Position the center mushroom slightly higher than the two on the sides. Insert the side mushroom pieces at an angle to form a fan shape.

4. Insert the pheasant feathers in front of the mushroom pieces, forming another semicircle or fan shape.

5. Insert the dried okra pieces, allowing them to form a horizontal "S" shape, going left to right in front of the feathers.

6. Insert the dried poppy pods in the spaces between the okra pieces.

7. Insert the remaining dried mushroom pieces down the front of the moss-covered cone, creating a triangle. Insert two side-by-side, below the okra and poppy pods, being sure to cover the bases of the stems, then insert the third mushroom just below the other two. Insert the mushrooms deeply into the moss-covered cone to be sure that none of the wooden stems are exposed.

Wheat Swag

This swag can be made quickly and easily with the help of an S-shaped grapevine swag.

Designed by Sherry Bartman
Difficulty level: Easy

YOU WILL NEED

S-shaped grapevine swag form
30 wheat stalks
10 small cattails
10 pheasant feathers
Bunch of sweet Annie, red
½" wide wire-edge ribbon, green, red, and yellow
1¾" wide satin ribbon, multi-colored
Hot glue gun and glue sticks

1 Use hot glue to secure the wheat stalks to the swag, following the curves of the "S" shape for placement. Reserve about 10 stalks for Step 5.

2 Use hot glue to attach the cattails to the swag, following the shape of the swag. Use about five cattails on each side.

3 Attach five pheasant feathers to each side of the swag, having them point directly out from the middle of the swag, not curving up the "S" shape.

4 Divide the bunch of sweet Annie in half. Fill in the design with sweet Annie, using about half on each side. Some of the sweet Annie can follow the "S" shape, while some can follow the pheasant feathers, giving length to the design.

5 Tie the 1¾" ribbon around the center of the swag. Make a multi-loop bow. Slip the remaining wheat stalks into the middle loop of the bow. Secure with hot glue, if needed.

6 Using the three pieces of ½" ribbon together, make a multi-loop bow. Secure to the multi-loop bow made in Step 5 with hot glue. Curl the ribbon ends.

Autumn Harvest Topiary

Designed by Edwin R. Smith
Difficulty level: Intermediate

YOU WILL NEED

Coffee cup
STYROFOAM® brand foam: 15" x 4" cone and 4" x
    4" x 2" sheet
8" tall urn*
Spray paint, copper and cherry wood
Craft foil, 8½" x 12" sheets, copper and gold
20 yds. of 24 gauge brass wire
Green sheet moss
Assorted autumn florals pods, berries, and leaves
Natural raffia
Fabric leaf
1½" straight pins
U pins
Craft foam, embossing tool or blunt pencil, knife, low-
    temperature glue gun and glue sticks, paper towels,
    pencil, scissors, wire cutters

*Used in this project: Timeless Accents Classic Urn
(BRC80004); Design Master® Copper spray 733 and
Cherry Wood Tone spray 756; Reynolds® Ultra Foil™.

Covered with fruits, nuts, and metallic leaves,
this topiary can adorn any tabletop or mantle.

❶ In a well-ventilated area and following the manufacturer's directions, spray the urn with two coats of copper,
allowing the paint to dry after each coat coat. Lightly mist
the dry urn with cherry wood tone. Allow to dry.
❷ With a pencil, trace around the leaf pattern on the
copper and gold foil. Trace about nine of each color. Cut
out.
❸ Working on craft foam, emboss veins in each of the
leaves with the embossing tool. Use strong, firm pressure
to make deep embossed lines.
❹ In a well-ventilated area, spray the leaves with cherry
wood tone. While still damp, lightly wipe with a paper
towel, leaving some of the color on each leaf. Spray and
wipe both sides of each leaf. Allow to dry.
❺ Cover the cone with moss, holding it in place with U pins.
❻ Wrap the moss-covered cone with brass wire in a
random pattern. Fasten the ends of wire with U pins.
❼ With a knife, trim the foam sheet to fit inside of the urn.
Glue in place. Glue the moss-covered cone into the urn.
❽ Shape the foil leaves into gentle curves. Using the
photo as a guide, pin and glue the leaves to the cone. Use
the gold and copper leaves at random, turning some leaves
to show the silver underside.
❾ Attach raffia to the cone with U pins, allowing the raffia
to flow through the design.
❿ Insert and glue the other floral material to the cone,
starting with the largest and ending with the smallest. Use
a variety of colors and sizes for the most visual interest.

Harvest Basket

Designed by Edwin R. Smith
Difficulty level: Advanced

This basket is a rendition of the traditional Thanksgiving cornucopia. Fill it with whatever fruits and vegetables you'd like.

YOU WILL NEED

14" long x 6" tall x 7" wide wicker basket*
12" long x 12" tall x 2" wide floral foam**
25 stems natural bearded wheat
3 sponge mushrooms
Large grape cluster, burgundy
2 pear, green pears
4 assorted apples
2 dried artichokes, green
4 berry sprays, autumn colors
Assorted autumn leaves
3 yds. 3" wide ribbon, natural
3 wood floral picks
Reindeer moss, green
Sheet moss, green
Floral U pins, floral wire (24 gauge), heavy white craft glue
    or hot glue gun and glue sticks, knife, plastic garbage
    bag, ruler, scissors, wire cutters

*Note: For a centerpiece, choose a basket that will be no more than 12" tall when filled, so guests can easily see over it.

**Used in this project: STYROFOAM brand foam.

Tip
Gluing a floral pick in each fruit allows for easier placement in the design.

❶ Line the basket with the garbage bag (this keeps any moss from falling from the basket when the design is complete and helps hide the foam). Cut the foam to fit inside the basket. Glue it in place, and secure with floral wire by crossing over the top of the foam. Cover the foam with sheet moss, holding it in place with floral U pins.
❷ Cluster the wheat into a bunch and place it across the top of the foam in a diagonal line. Secure with floral U pins and glue. Insert one sponge mushroom through the basket, near the base on the front right. Glue in place. Insert two sponge mushrooms, overlapping and extending over the edge of the basket on the right side.
❸ Puncture a small hole in the bottom of a pear. Insert a floral pick into the hole, and glue it in place. Insert picks into each piece of fruit, varying the insertion point of the pick so some fruits will be on their side. Insert a picked pear to the right of the basket handle, near the basket edge. Glue the second pear behind the first.
❹ Cut the grape cluster into two sections. Attach a floral pick to each section. Insert one grape cluster to the left of the basket handle, cascading over the edge of the basket. Insert the other grape cluster on the opposite side of the basket. Using the photo as a guide, insert and glue the fruit into the design. Start with the larger fruit and end with the smaller pieces.
❺ Insert the leaves, extending over the right and left ends of the basket. Shape the leaves into natural-looking curves that flow downward. Cut the berry sprays into assorted lengths and insert into the design, as shown. Shape the berries to create a sense of movement. Glue a small cluster of reindeer moss to fill the spaces between the fruit and to hide any glue. Glue a small cluster of moss and berries to the sponge mushroom at the base of the basket.
❻ Look at the design from all sides to make sure it appears balanced. Adjust the fruits, berries, and moss as needed.
❼ Cut the ribbon into three 12" lengths and form the pieces into loops secured with floral wire. Insert the ribbon pieces into the design to fill any spaces between the fruits. Use the rest of the ribbon to form streamers that flow over the edge of the basket. Trim the ribbon ends into a V shape. Add more moss as needed to fill in and hide any glue.

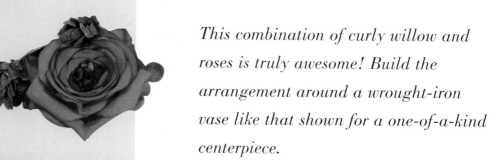

Awesome
Autumn Vase

Designed by Gail Gregor
Difficulty level: Advanced

YOU WILL NEED

Wrought-iron vase
1 bunch fresh curly willow branches
2" tall x 4" diameter foam disk
Sheet or decorator moss
2 artificial apples, green
5 clusters grapes, green
2 stems roses, bright orange
3 stems roses, rust
2 stems rosebuds, rust
3 stems roses, red
2 stems rosebuds, red
5 stems English lavender
3 stems hops, rust
Awl or other sharp tool (optional), brown floral tape, greening pins, hot glue gun and glue sticks, pliers, wire (18 or 20 gauge), wire cutters, wood picks (3" to 4" long)

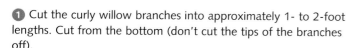

This combination of curly willow and roses is truly awesome! Build the arrangement around a wrought-iron vase like that shown for a one-of-a-kind centerpiece.

1 Cut the curly willow branches into approximately 1- to 2-foot lengths. Cut from the bottom (don't cut the tips of the branches off).

2 Cover the wire with brown floral tape.

3 Place the willow branches into the vase. Take one branch and place it near the base of the vase. Secure that branch to the vase with the covered wire and pliers and then weave the remainder of the branch in and out of the vase's open areas in a freeform pattern. Insert all the branches, beginning at the base of the vase, in a spiral that goes in one direction to resemble a bird's nest. Use more wire, if necessary, to hold the branches in place.

4 Add a few small branches to the base of the container, as in Step 3.

5 Cover the foam disk with sheet moss on all sides. Secure with greening pins. Place the moss-covered disk in the center of the vase. Use the covered wire to attach the disk to the vase. Make sure the disk won't move after you've wired it.

6 Begin the design with the orange roses. Trim one rose's stem to 2". Glue it to the foam disk, at the front of the vase. Insert the other orange rose, with a stem about 3" long, into the back of the design.

7 Cut the rust-colored roses to about 4" or 5". Insert one between the two orange roses, the second to the back and toward the right, and the third should through the rungs of the vase hanging down toward the front left.

8 Cut one red rose to about 3" or 4" and one to 5" or 6". Insert the shorter rose near the back and left, and the second spiraling out from the back of the vase toward the front. Cut the stem completely from the final rose, and glue it to one of the front feet of the vase.

9 Make a hole in the side of one of the apples using a wood pick. If the apple is too firm, make a hole with an awl or other sharp tool and then insert the wood pick. Glue the pick into the apple. Insert and glue the apple into the design to the left of the rust and orange roses. Place the second apple on the right side of the vase, near the base. **Note:** You may need to glue the apple to the willow to secure it.

10 Cut the red rosebud stems to approximately 6" to 7". Insert one on the right side of the arrangement, behind the rust-colored rose. The second can be added as desired.

11 Use the rust-colored rosebuds, English lavender, and hops to fill in the design as needed. You can add these stems in a spiral pattern where necessary.

12 Attach one grape cluster near the apple at the base of the vase, one near the rust-colored rose in the front, and one near the green apple inside the vase. The other two may be positioned and glued in place where needed.

13 Check the design. Make sure the foam is covered completely and that all of the stems are glued firmly in place.

Sunflower Wreath

Tiny terra cotta pots and seed packets add an interesting touch to this easy-to-make wreath.

Designed by Sherry Bartman
Difficulty level: Easy

YOU WILL NEED

Twig wreath form (with twigs extending)
About 50 silk leaves, fall and ivy
Sunflower bush
4 small terra cotta pots
3 seed packets
3 pods
Baby's breath, green
Spanish moss
Hot glue gun and glue sticks, wire cutters

❶ Insert the baby's breath into the wreath, following the lines of the extended twigs. If needed, secure with hot glue.

❷ Attach the fall and ivy leaves to the wreath. Cut the stems on some very short and attach directly to the wreath and leave some stems longer to follow the lines of the extended twigs and baby's breath. Reserve some leaves to fill in the design in Step 5.

❸ Mentally divide the wreath in half, top and bottom. You will be designing on the bottom half of the wreath. Clip the sunflower bush apart and insert the sunflowers evenly around the bottom portion of the wreath.

❹ Put a little Spanish moss into each of the terra cotta pots. Secure with glue, if needed. Using glue, evenly attach the seed packets, terra cotta pots, and pods to the bottom portion of the wreath, amongst the sunflowers.

❺ If needed, fill in the design with the remaining leaves.

Natural Elegance Arrangement

Designed by Lisa Galvin
Difficulty level: Easy

These flowers appear as though they are growing right out of the container!

YOU WILL NEED

9¼" bowl, dark purple*
2" x 4" piece of floral foam, green with adhesive
1 stem antique roses x 3, burgundy
1 stem antique larkspur, gold/rust
1 stem coneflower x 3, ivory
2 aster sprays x 4, peach
Ming moss
Sheet moss
Cool-temp glue gun and glue sticks, ruler, wire
   cutters

*Used in this project: Syndicate Sales Round Lotus Bowl #62, Berry, Plastifoam ball.

Tip
Using more than one type of moss or filler material tends to give an arrangement a more natural appearance. There is a variety of floral mosses to choose from, and most can be found at local craft stores and florists.

❶ Peal the paper from the square piece of foam. Apply a ring of glue around the square and firmly press to the center of the bowl.

❷ Establish the design lines by working from the back of the arrangement. Divide one larkspur stem into two separate stems by cutting it approximately 18" down the stem with wire cutters, near the emerging flowers on the lower stem section. Leave a tiny stub of stem wire exposed and create a second stem to add to the arrangement later. The flowers remaining on the bottom portion of the original stem easily conceal the wire stub. Insert the top larkspur stem into the foam at the back of the arrangement.

❸ Bend a rose stem slightly for a natural appearance, cut it to the desired length, and insert it into the foam to the side and in front of the larkspur.

❹ Cut the coneflower stems to separate them, and insert into the foam.

❺ Conceal the foam base by gluing sheet moss around the inserted stems and into the bowl.

❻ Insert the aster sprays and remaining larkspur stem into the foam, near the center.

❼ Fill in around the base with mosses.

Magnolia and Apple Wreath

Designed by Edwin R. Smith
Difficulty level: Easy

Covered with fall berries and crab apples, this wreath can be hung on a wall or used as a centerpiece with a candle set in the middle.

YOU WILL NEED

12" x 2" foam wreath, white*
30 magnolia leaves, silk or preserved
36 crab apples, assorted colors
75 berries, red
75 cranberries, rust and red
1½ yds. 2½" wide ribbon, dark green
Chenille stem, floral U pins, heavy white craft glue or low-temp glue gun and glue sticks, scissors, 2" straight pins, wire cutter
*Used in this project: STYROFOAM brand foam.

❶ Glue the ribbon around the outside edge of the wreath. Trim the ribbon even with the wreath edges.

❷ Shape the magnolia leaves into gentle curves. Glue them to the inside edges of the wreath and secure with straight pins, if needed. The leaves overlap slightly and extend beyond the wreath on both the inside and out.

❸ Turn the wreath upside down and pin and glue a row of leaves to the back of the wreath as in Step 2. Turn the wreath over and adjust and add leaves, as needed to create symmetry.

❹ Glue two rows of crab apples on the face of the wreath, alternating colors and their positions. Glue clusters of red berries between the crab apples. Glue the cranberries around the opening of the wreath, near the crab apples.

❺ Twist the chenille stem into a loop. Insert it in the top back of the wreath as a hanger. Secure with floral U pins.

Witch Hat

Designed by Edwin R. Smith
Difficulty level: Intermediate

This eerily elegant Halloween arrangement will look great hanging from a wall or door.

YOU WILL NEED

9" x 5" foam cone*
10" x 8" rectangle of ¼" foam core or heavy cardboard, black
2 pompoms, 2", black
8" bump chenille stem, 15mm, black
12" chenille stem, black (optional)
2 mums with leaves, orange
2 berry sprays, orange
12" long twigs
2 yds. 1½" wide sheer ribbon, purple
4 yds. satin ribbon, orange
3 acrylic gems, clear
4 pompoms, 10mm, neon green
1" pearl pins, black
Flat spray paint*, black
Spray paint*, purple
Spray adhesive*
Glitter, black and green
Compass, craft knife, ruler, scissors, thick white craft glue, wire cutters, wood skewer

*Used in this project: STYROFOAM brand foam; Design Master® spray paint and Tack 2000.

1 Using the compass, trace a 9" diameter circle onto the foam core or cardboard. Cut the circle out with the craft knife. Measure in 3" from one edge of the circle and draw a straight line across the circle. Cut along the line to create a circle with one straight edge.

2 Glue the cut circle to the base of the foam cone with one edge of the cone base centered on and flush with the straight line to form the hat.

3 Insert the wood skewer into the tip of the cone until it is not seen. This helps keep the cone from breaking. In a well-ventilated area, spray the hat with two coats of black paint. Let dry between coats. Spray the twigs purple. Let dry.

4 Following the manufacturer's directions, spray the hat with spray adhesive and sprinkle with black and green glitter. Repeat if necessary to completely cover the hat. Let dry.

5 Optional: Twist the 12" long chenille stem into a loop. Insert the loop into the back side of the cone, about 5" below the tip to form a hanger. Glue in place. Adjust the hanger as needed so the hat hangs against the wall.

6 Glue the orange satin ribbon around the edge of the hat brim. Glue the purple ribbon around the base of the hat as a hatband. Repeat with the orange ribbon.

7 Glue the purple twigs to the left side of the hat, extending both upward and downward. Cut one mum to 5" and glue to the left side of the hat, near the twigs. Cut the other mum to 2"

and glue at the base of the other mum and twigs. Glue the leaves and berry sprays around the mums and twigs.

8 Glue loops of purple ribbon to cascade over the left edge of the hat with streamers about 12" long. Using the photo as a guide, glue the loops to the underside of the hat brim. Repeat with the orange ribbon. Trim the ends of the purple ribbon in a "V" cut. Glue the acrylic gems to the ribbons as desired.

9 Cut the bump chenille stems into two bump sections for a total of sixteen sections. Fold and twist each section to form a spider leg. Glue eight legs equally spaced around the base of each pompom. Glue the neon green pompoms to the black pompoms as spider eyes. Insert and glue the black pearl pins to the center of each green pompom.

10 Glue one spider to the right brim of the hat and the second spider in the loop of purple ribbon on the underside of the hat brim.

Cat Pumpkin

Designed by Kim Wakefield
Difficulty level: Easy

There's no need to be superstitious of this black cat!

YOU WILL NEED

13½" carveable foam pumpkin
Cat cutout kit*
Oak leaf garland
Small fall mum bush, orange
Mixed floral/berries/nuts fall bush
Spanish moss
Raffia, natural
Foam block
Greening pins, hot glue gun and glue sticks, scissors, serrated knife, wire cutters.

*Pumpkin Buddies cat cutout kit was used in this project.

1 Cut out and remove an oval section on the front of the pumpkin.
2 Use the serrated knife to cut the foam block to fit in the pumpkin. Glue in place. Glue moss over the foam to cover.
3 Following the manufacturer's instructions, insert the Pumpkin Buddies cat's head, paws, and tail in the pumpkin.
4 Wrap the garland around the sides and top of the pumpkin. Secure with greening pins. Cut off and set any excess aside.
5 Cut the bushes apart and arrange into the foam as desired. Fill in empty spaces with extra garland pieces.
6 Tie a raffia bow, and glue on the top of the pumpkin.

Snowman Candy Land, page 76

CHAPTER FOUR

Winter

The winter holidays are a time for elegant décor and jubilant celebrations. For most of the country, the ground, trees, and buildings are covered in a peaceful snow that chases us closer to warm roasts and crackling fires.

Flowers should reflect the peace and joy of togetherness. Orchids, roses, and violets are a few favorites. Weave them into a Christmas wreath to hang on your door, or create several and use a wreath theme to decorate an empty wall.

Candles are also a common sight, and they invite numerous design possibilities. Floral wreaths surround them, candy canes support them, and they appear by themselves as molded snowmen and Christmas trees.

Winter just isn't the same without all the wonderful smells and tastes of candy, cookies, and other luscious desserts. Incorporate a candy dish into your arrangement, or decorate a gingerbread house to replace a candle or large focal flowers.

Other winter flowers include: heather, anemones, amaryllis, and camellia flowers. Use mistletoe and pine boughs as filler.

IN THIS CHAPTER

Snowflake, Twig, and Candle Centerpiece

Designed by Edwin R. Smith
Difficulty level: Easy

Glittery white twigs surround a bowl that can contain a floating candle, candy, ornaments, or anything else you desire.

YOU WILL NEED

14" x 2" foam wreath*
Shallow clear glass bowl with 8" opening (the bowl must fit inside the wreath opening)
Grapevine
36 birch or other twigs, 18" long
3 snowflakes, 5½"
7 snowflakes, 4"
10 zinnias, white
Clusters of wax flowers, white
Ivy leaves
3 yds. sheer ribbon 2" wide, white
3 yds. ribbon ¾" wide, silver
Floating candle
Glass gems or marbles*
Spray paint, silver and white
Floral U pins, floral wire (24 gauge), heavy white craft glue or low-temp glue gun and glue sticks, ruler, scissors, wire cutters

*Used in this project: Styrofoam brand foam; Design Master.

Tip
Be sure to use spray paint that is safe for foam. Some paints can melt foam, so check the paint manufacturer's packaging.

❶ In a well-ventilated area, lightly spray the foam wreath, grapevine, and twigs with silver paint, allowing to dry. Spray the twigs and grapevine with two or more coats of white paint until well coated. Let dry.

❷ Loosely wrap the grapevine around the foam wreath, pinning in place with floral U pins. Adjust the grapevine so the wreath sits level on a table. Dip the ends of the twigs one at a time into glue and insert into the top of the wreath, to a height of about 14" to 16". Create five clusters of twigs equally spaced around the wreath. Spray the twigs and grapevine white again. Let dry.

❸ Cut the white ribbon into three 1-yard lengths. Loosely weave the ribbon lengths though the grapevine and around the base of the twig clusters, securing in place with floral U pins.

❹ Using the photo as a guide, cut the zinnias into short stem lengths and insert and glue into the base of the twig clusters. Glue ivy leaves at the base of the flowers. Insert and glue small clusters of wax flowers around the zinnias. Form 12" lengths of silver ribbon into loops. Secure with floral wire. Insert the silver loop into the design, as desired.

❺ Place the glass bowl in the center of the wreath, adjusting the twigs, grapevine, and ribbon as needed. Insert the snowflakes into the design. Place some at the base of the twigs and some in the twig clusters.

❻ Place the glass gems in the bottom of the bowl. Fill the bowl with water and add the floating candle. Use caution when burning the candle so that all flammable materials are away from the flame. Never leave a burning candle unattended!

Old World Elegance Candle Stands

Decorated candle stands can add the perfect touch to a holiday dinner table or fireplace mantel. For a distinct holiday flavor, use vellum and gold foil to add ornaments to hang from the garland.

Designed by Lisa Galvin
Difficulty level: Intermediate

Another Idea

Try making vellum ornaments to hang from the candle stands! Cut the vellum into an oval, punch and emboss it as desired, and add gold foil embellishments. Use wire to make a small hanger at the top of each ornament. To hang the ornaments, create small hooks and attach them to the foam disks on the candle stands. Hook the ornaments onto the foam disks. The ornaments shown were created with Fiskars shape templates, cutters, and crimpers, Reynolds Bright Ideas gold Ultra Foil, and gold vellum.

YOU WILL NEED

2 wood-tone candle stands, 8"
2 candles, 12", amber/gold-tone
2 foam disks, 4" x 1"*
6 floral picks, small grape clusters with leaves
Assorted evergreen stems/branches floral picks
20 and 24 gauge craft wire, gold*
Bugle beads, gold
6mm simulated pearl beads
Simulated pearl teardrop beads
6 jewelry bell caps
Floral wire, green
Floral moss
Foam craft sheet
Two ¾" sequin pins, gold
Pencil, wire cutters

*Used in this project: Syndicate Sales Plastifoam The Fun Starts Here! Disks; The Beadery® wire.

❶ Cut a 24" piece of 24 gauge gold wire. Fold one end back approximately 1" and twist it with the remaining length of wire so that beads won't slip off. Slip beads onto the wire in the following order: 10 bugle beads, 6mm pearl, 10 bugle beads, teardrop pearl. Repeat, adding additional beads until you are within 1½" from the wire end. Fold the end back and twist to secure, holding the beads in place. Repeat the process so that you have two beaded pieces of wire.

❷ Turn the candle stand upside down and press the top into the center of each foam disk, twisting to indent the foam slightly. This will be the bottom of the candle ring. Remove.

❸ Roll the outer edges of foam onto a hard surface to round off the hard cut lines. Insert a pencil into the center of the foam to create a hole. Use a pencil to press the side edges, creating a hole that the candle will easily slip through. Cover the foam with moss, wrapping with floral wire to hold it in place.

❹ Use wire cutters to cut evergreen "stems" and grape clusters/leaves from the floral picks. Insert the evergreen stems into the moss-covered foam, curving the stems to encircle the disk. Insert the grape clusters and leaves, arranging them around the disk. Repeat for the remaining candle stand.

❺ Place the candle rings onto the candle stands, pressing the indented foam edge onto the stand for added stability.

❻ Insert the candle through the candle ring (disk) and into the stand. Insert the long wire end of the beaded garland made in Step 1 into the foam and wrap, spiraling upward around candle, securing at the top with a gold sequin pin.

Frosty Centerpiece

A gold wreath and iced fruit are the perfect partners for a frosted vase that can hold a pillar candle or additional fruit. The vase's look is achieved with Crystal Creations, which can be washed away with soap and water, so you can reapply as needed and remove the crystals to take your glass container from winter to spring.

Designed by Kristy McNeil
Difficulty level: Easy

YOU WILL NEED

Syndicate Sales Crystal Creations™
Large opening vase*
Iced fruit floral spray
Iced berries stem
6" grapevine wreath
Spray paint, gold
6" tall pillar candle
Floral wire (28 gauge), hair dryer

*Used in this project: Syndicate Sales vase #4111; Design Master 24kt Gold Paint

❶ Spray the Crystal Creations approximately 6" to 8" from the vase. Turn the hair dryer on low and keep at a distance from the glass—watch the crystals form. Play with the crystals until the desired look is achieved.

❷ Remove the large binding grapevine from the wreath. Loosen the wreath to allow the vase to sit in the center.

❸ Following the manufacturer's directions, spray the wreath gold.

❹ Clip the flowers from the spray and wire to the wreath as desired. Add the berries.

❺ Set the vase in the center of the wreath and add the candle.

Antique Rose Mirror

Designed by Elaine Schmidt
Difficulty level: Intermediate

YOU WILL NEED

20" x 24" purchased mirror with gold frame
4 antique rose sprays, cream
2 large antique roses, cream
1 dried silk eucalyptus spray
1 burrberry spray
3¼ yds. 3" wide wire-edge ribbon, cream
3 yds. 1½" wide mesh wire-edge ribbon, gold
3 yds. ⅞" wide wire-edge ribbon, cream/gold
3 strands beads, crystal and gold
22 gauge wire, non-tarnish gold
Metallic spray paint, gold
Brown floral tape, hot glue gun and glue sticks, round
   nose pliers

Silk flowers, ribbon, and crystal beads embellish this elegant home décor accent.

❶ Following the manufacturer's directions, very lightly spray all of the florals with gold metallic paint.

❷ Holding the gold mesh and cream/gold ribbons together, make a six-loop bow with long streamers. Glue the bow to the lower left corner of the mirror.

❸ Arrange all of the florals along the left and bottom sides of the mirror and glue to hold.

❹ To make the bead clusters, cut 30" pieces of wire, each 6" long. Curl one end of each wire into a loop and curl the wire into a spiral. On 18" pieces of the spiraled wire, thread on various crystal beads. Make six bead clusters by taking three wires with beads and two wires without and twisting them together. Wrap the ends of the wires with floral tape.

❺ Position the bead clusters amongst the flowers and glue to hold.

❻ To make the bow, cut a 2-yard length of the cream ribbon. Make a six-loop bow with no streamers. Use wire in the center to hold. Cut a 3" length of the ribbon and glue it over the center of the bow to hid the wire. Cut the remaining ribbon in half and glue the streamers out from the back of the bow. Make a small wire loop and glue it to the back of the bow.

❼ Position the bow above the mirror, making sure that the streamers are placed an equal distance from the edge of the mirror. Glue to hold.

Caution!
When hanging the mirror, use the hanging device that is on the back of the mirror! The picture bow is not strong enough to hold the weight of the mirror. Once the mirror is hung, hang the bow on a nail above, giving the illusion that it is holding up the mirror.

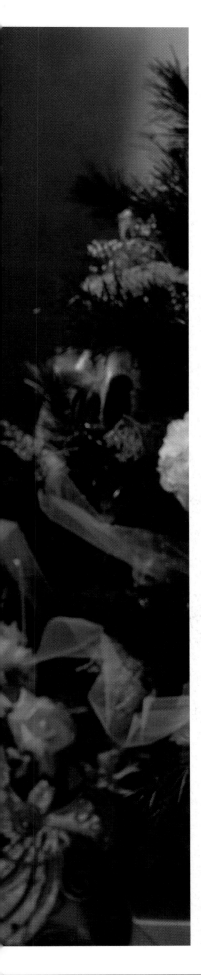

Victorian Floral Centerpiece

This rose-bedecked pine wreath gets a royal treatment when ornaments, a hurricane globe, and a candle are added.

Designed by Kim Wakefield
Difficulty level: Easy

YOU WILL NEED

Pre-made pine and pink roses wreath*
Glass hurricane globe
2 bolts sheer ribbon, 3 yds. each, ivory
Christmas ornaments: 3 sheet music, 4 white flower balls,
    7 assorted beaded fruits
Medium English ivy bush
5 sheer and silk roses, cream with gold glitter edges*
Pillar candle, ivory with gold dot accents
Craft foam sheet
Floral wire (26 gauge), hot glue gun and glue sticks, scissors, serrated knife, wire cutter

*Used in this project: Holiday Elegance wreath, roses; Crystalite ribbon.

1 Use the knife to cut the foam to fit snugly in the center of the wreath. Secure with glue and floral wire. Arrange the pine branches to "fluff" the wreath.

2 Randomly hot-glue ornaments around the wreath. Cut all but 1" of stem from the cream roses. Hot-glue the roses evenly around the wreath.

3 Make a multi-loop bow with long streamers from sheer ribbon. Use floral wire to secure onto the wreath. Weave the streamers in and around the entire wreath, tucking them into the arrangement to hold.

4 Glue the hurricane globe on the foam in the center of the wreath.

5 Cut apart all of the ivy bush stems. Hot-glue the pieces throughout the wreath. Let a few longer pieces trail upward around the globe.

6 Insert the candle into the globe.

Snowman Candy Land

Designed by Edwin R. Smith
Difficulty level: Easy

Various types and sizes of foam are combined to make this cheerful Christmas candy dish that can be displayed all winter long.

YOU WILL NEED

12" foam disk*
10" foam extruded wreath*
Foam balls: 2 balls 3", 3 balls 2", 2 balls 1½", 8 balls 1"*
2 top hats, 2½", black
1½" pearl-head pins, black
24" of 1¼" wide ribbon, red plaid
2 yds. 2½" wide ribbon, white iridescent
2 snowflakes, 4"
8 snowflakes, 3½"
Snow branch
Assorted evergreens, snowy and plain
3 berry sprays, 12", silver
Birch or other twigs
Glitter, iridescent
Acrylic paint, orange
Wrapped candy of choice
Cotton swab, floral wire (24 gauge), heavy white craft
   glue, knife, ruler, scissors, toothpicks, wire cutters

*Used in this project: STYROFOAM brand foam.

❶ Using the knife, bevel the edge of the foam disk. Smooth the edge with a scrap of foam, using it as sandpaper. Insert three toothpicks into one side of the wreath. Apply glue to the picked side and place it on top of the beveled disk, off-center. **Note:** The toothpicks help hold the wreath in place.

❷ To make the snowmen, cut small slices from each of the 3" foam balls so they lie flat. Use a toothpick to attach a 1½" ball on top of a 2½" ball, and glue in place. Use a toothpick to attach the 2½" ball to the top of a 3" ball, and glue in place. Repeat for the second snowman. Cut a 2½" ball into quarters. Gently squeeze and compress each cut section into snowman arms. Glue the arms to the snowmen.

❸ Use a toothpick to attach a snowman on top of the foam disk, at left. Glue it in place. Repeat to place the other snowman on the lower right side of the disk. Dip an end of a cotton swab into orange acrylic paint. Let dry. Dip the tips of the pins one at a time into glue and insert into the snowmen for buttons and facial features. Cut the pins shorter with wire cutters, if needed, so that they do not protrude from the foam. Cut the orange ends from the swabs and insert and glue into the snowmen for noses. Cut the red plaid ribbon into 12" lengths. Wrap one length of ribbon around each snowman as a scarf, gluing in place. Fringe the end of each ribbon. Glue a hat onto each snowman.

❹ Cut the evergreens into short lengths. Using the photo as a guide, insert and glue evergreens around each snowman. Insert and glue twigs behind and to the right of the top snowman and to the left of the bottom snowman.

❺ Cut one berry spray in half and vertically insert one section into each group of twigs. Cut the other berry sprays into short lengths and insert around each snowman. Using the photo as a guide, insert and glue snowflakes to the design.

❻ Cut the white ribbon into 12" lengths. Form it into loops, secure with floral wire. Insert the loops into the design as desired. Trim the end of the ribbon into "V" shapes.

❼ Glue 1" foam balls at random to the design.

❽ Apply a light coat of glue to each snowman's hat, scarf, and body. Sprinkle with glitter.

❾ Place wrapped candy inside of the wreath.

Red and White Christmas Wreath

Designed by Edwin R. Smith
Difficulty level: Easy

YOU WILL NEED

14" x 2" foam wreath*
75 glass stem balls, 30mm, red
75 satin glass stem balls, 30mm, white
20 glass stem balls, 25mm, red
5 yds. 2¾" wide wire-edge velvet ribbon, red
Evergreen sprigs
Chenille stem, floral wire (24 gauge), floral U pins, heavy white craft glue*, scissors, wire cutters

*Used in this project: STYROFOAM brand foam; Beacon Kids Choice Glue™.

The beauty of this wreath lies in its pure simple elegance.

❶ Using wire cutters, clip the wire stems to about 1" lengths on the glass balls. Starting at the bottom mid-point of the wreath, dip the stems of the larger (30mm) red balls into glue and insert into the wreath, creating a diagonal red row. The balls should be placed as close together as possible and should cover the top and sides of the wreath.

❷ Create a diagonal row of white balls, as you did with the red, making sure the balls form even lines and the balls are as close together as possible. Continue around the wreath, alternating colors until the wreath is completely covered.

❸ Form a multi-loop bow with the red velvet ribbon. The loops should be about 4½". Secure the bow with floral wire. Insert the wire into the top of the wreath, securing it with glue. Add extra streamers, if needed. Pin the bow with floral U pins, if needed, to hold in place. The bow should sit near the top edge of the wreath. Trim the ends of the streamers into "V" shapes.

❹ Dip the ends of the evergreen sprigs into glue. Insert the sprigs between the balls, to fill in any open spaces. Add smaller (25mm) red balls as accents throughout the wreath.

❺ Glue sprigs of evergreen in and around the bow. Glue glass balls in the bow, as desired.

❻ Twist the chenille stem into a loop. Insert it into the top back of the wreath as a hanger. Secure with floral U pins and glue.

Candy Cane Candleholder

Designed by Edwin R. Smith
Difficulty level: Easy

The artificial candies used to embellish this candleholder look almost good enough to eat!

YOU WILL NEED

7¾" x 6¾" x 2" foam vase, green*
7½" x 1¼" foam disk, white*
30 cellophane-wrapped candy canes, 6"
5 yds. 1½" wide ribbon, red
6" tall pillar candle, red
9" x 12" piece of felt, green
Assorted Christmas greens/pine, plain and frosted
Artificial candy, red and white striped
Berry clusters, red
Pinecones, frosted
Floral wire (24 gauge), low-temp glue gun and glue
  sticks or heavy white craft glue*, pencil, scissors, wire
  cutters

*Used in this project: STYROFOAM brand foam; Beacon
Kids Choice Glue.

Caution!
Never leave a burning candle unattended!

❶ Place the foam disk on the green felt and trace around it. Cut out the felt circle and glue it onto the disk. Place the round end of the vase insert on the green felt, and trace around it. Cut out the felt circle, and glue it on the round end of the vase insert. Glue red ribbon around the side of the disk, trimming to fit.

❷ Place the round end of the vase insert up and glue it to the center of the disk, with the felt side of the disk down. The felt will protect furniture from scratches.

❸ Glue the candy canes around the sides of the vase insert so that the tops of the canes are level with the top of the vase insert. Glue the canes as close together as possible.

❹ Using wire cutters, cut the pin and Christmas greens into short lengths. Using the photo as a guide, glue and insert greens around the bottom of the candy canes, forming a ring.

❺ Use the red ribbon to form a two-loop bow with loops of about 3". Secure the center of the bow with floral wire. Insert it into the greenery, and glue it in place.

❻ Glue the cones, berries, and candy equally spaced around the greenery ring. Glue small sprigs of greens, berries, and candy, as pictured, around the top of the candleholder.

❼ Place the candle on top of the holder, adjusting the greens, berries, and candies so that that candle sits level and secure.

Wire Leaves on Baskets, page 84

CHAPTER FIVE

Containers

While you're hunting for supplies and envisioning your flowers and vines, always keep the container in mind. You don't want your flowers to overwhelm your pot, and at the same time you don't want your pot to be more prominent than the arrangement. The elements should complement each other to make a balanced, eye-catching presentation. Many options are available. Choose from vases, crates, baskets, and pots. Then decide which materials appeal to you. Containers can be made with wire, glass, foil, wood, twigs, terra cotta, or polymer clay. They can be etched, engraved, carved, paper-covered, woven, or embellished with beads, paints, plaster, or fabrics.

If you exhaust your list of ideas, and you still haven't found the perfect complement for your favorite design, try something from the rummage sale box. An old boot, a hat that's seen better days, or a child's toy that hasn't been played with in years all can be modified to fit a floral arrangement.

IN THIS CHAPTER

Foil Vase

Foil spirals adhere to the inside of this fun vase.

Designed by Debba Haupert
Difficulty level: Easy

YOU WILL NEED

Craft foil, red and green*
Double-sided adhesive sheets*
9" tall glass vase*
Decorative-edge scissors*
Scissors, paper cutter, or rotary cutting equipment
Soft cloth or cork

*Used in this project: AMACO® ArtEmboss Foil, Bright Red and Mint Green; Therm O Web Keep a Memory double-sided adhesive; Syndicate Sales Trumpet Vase; Fiskars Deckle scissors.

1 Make sure your vase is clean and dry.

2 Cut a 1-foot long piece of red foil. Peel one side from the double-sided adhesive sheet and apply to the color side of the foil. With the decorative-edge scissors, cut numerous circles ranging from 2" to 3" wide. Cut a spiral in the circles to the center. Starting at the tail of the first spiral, cut another spiral that also meets in the center, creating two spirals. **Note:** You'll cut down the center of the spiral to meet at the center. Alternate going clockwise and counter-clockwise to alter the spirals' direction.

3 Peel the back from the spirals and apply to the inside of the vase, with the red color facing out. The spirals can touch and overlap as desired. Rub the foil onto the vase with your fingers, a soft cloth, or a cork to give a clean adhesion to the glass.

4 Repeat Step 1 with the green foil. However, cut the green into leaf shapes (roughly 2" x 3"). Cut the leaves twice to create spiral leaves. Peel the adhesive backing and apply to the vase, behind the roses. Apply as many leaves as desired.

Acetone-Washed Foil Vase

Designed by Debba Haupert
Difficulty level: Intermediate

Applying acetone to craft foil gives the foil a unique, aged appearance.

YOU WILL NEED

Craft foil, violet, green, blue*
9" glass vase with straight sides
Double-sided adhesive sheets*
Acetone in a spray bottle
Leaf border punch*
Scissors, paper cutter, or rotary cutting equipment
Brayer (optional)

*Used in this project: AMACO ArtEmboss Foil, Violet, Sea Green, Cerulean Blue; Therm O Web PeelnStick double-sided adhesive sheets; Fiskars Leaf Border Punch.

Using Acetone
Acetone is available in hardware stores, near the paint supplies. Use caution when working with acetone, following the manufacturer's instructions.

❶ Cut each color of foil to 1-foot lengths. Try to avoid wrinkles and bends in the foil. If they appear, smooth them out with your hand or a brayer.

❷ Spray acetone onto two colored pieces of foil and place the color sides together. Allow the acetone to dry for 5 to 10 minutes. The foil colors will blend together. Pull the foils apart and repeat with the remaining foils, so each foil reacts with each of the other colors (violet/green, green/blue, blue/violet). Repeat as needed to mix the colors until you have achieved the desired color effect. **Note:** Some silver will show through.

❸ Cut the blue foil to a height of 9" and a width equal to the diameter of the vase plus 1". Punch along the top and bottom edges of the foil with the border punch. Cut double-sided adhesive to a height of 8" (to allow room for the punch holes) and a width equal to that of the blue foil. Pull off one side of the adhesive, and apply it to the center back of the foil. Roll the vase over the foil to attach, being careful to avoid wrinkles and to keep the foil even with the top and bottom edges of the vase.

❹ Cut the green foil to a height of 6" and a width equal to the diameter of the vase plus 1". Punch along the top and bottom edges of the foil. Cut the double-sided adhesive to a height of 5" and a width equal to that of the green foil. Pull off one side of the adhesive, and apply it to the center back of the foil. Carefully align the foil in the center of the vase, and roll the vase over the foil to attach. Keep the seam at the same point as the seam for the blue foil.

❺ Cut the violet foil to a height of 3" and a width equal to the diameter of the vase plus 1". Punch along the top and bottom edges of the foil. Cut the double-sided adhesive to a height of 2" and a width equal to that of the violet foil. Pull off one side of the adhesive, and apply it to the center back of the foil. Carefully align the foil in the center of the vase, and roll the vase over the foil to attach. Keep the seam at the same point as the seam for the green foil.

These simple twisted wire leaves can be used sparingly as the single branch on the bamboo basket, or in groups as in the green basket (page 80), with its wire vines encircling the basket. Don't worry if your wire color doesn't match your basket, because you can simply dab on some paint to change the color completely or just slightly, as in the bamboo basket.

Designed by Jane Davis
Difficulty level: Intermediate

YOU WILL NEED

Basket of any size, shape, and color
24" of 16 gauge wire for each 6" stem of leaves
24" of 24 or thinner gauge wire or tacky glue
Anvil, chain nose pliers, chasing hammer, round nose pliers, wire cutters

1 Using the round nose pliers, bend one end of the wire into a loop. Using your hands, and beginning 2" from the loop, loop the wire over itself into about a ½" loop and twist the wire at the base of the loop twice around. Make another loop in the same way, twisting in the opposite direction, so the wire forms a zigzag pattern with a loop at each change of direction. Make eight loops in all, four on each side.
2 Using the chain nose pliers, pinch each side of a loop, so that you create a point in the loop, making a leaf shape. Repeat for each loop.
3 Using the chasing hammer and anvil, pound the leaf tips flat.
4 Beginning at the tip of the branch, bend the segment of the stem toward the first leaf. Repeat for the next segment and leaf, making all of the leaves point toward the end of the branch.
5 Tuck the base of the branch into the basket. Either glue it in place at several places along the branch, or tie it to the basket with the thin wire.

Paper-Covered Vase

Designed by Andrea Rothenberg
Difficulty level: Intermediate

Punched paper lends a delicate touch to an otherwise plain bud vase.

YOU WILL NEED

7½" tall by 1¾" wide straight-sided bud vase*
Border punches*
Decorative-edge scissors*
Paper, burgundy*
Vellum, printed white*
Paper trimmer*
1" x 12" piece of craft foil, silver*
1" x 12" piece of double-sided adhesive
Laminating product*
Paintbrush

*Used in this project: Syndicate Sales; Fiskars® Flower and Diamond Border Punch, Scallop Paper Edgers, Country Colors paper, Vellum, Paper Trimmer; Reynolds Creative Essentials Bright Ideas Ultra™ Foil; Beacon Liquid Laminate™ All-In-One Laminating Product.

① Cut three strips of burgundy paper and vellum, each 1¼" x 7½".

② Slide one long edge of the burgundy paper into the flower border punch, making sure that the edge of the paper is firmly against the back wall of the punch. Punch. Slide the paper over and match up the punched design with the design silhouette that is printed on the base of the punch. Punch. Continue punching in this manner to create a continuous border along the length of the paper. Repeat for the remaining strips of paper.

③ Flip the paper so the opposite side can be punched. To line up the punched designs with the designs made in Step 2, use the raised notch in the center of the punch case. The flower is the center of this design, so it should be lined up under the notch as you slide the strip into the punch. Once the straight edge of the paper is against the back wall, punch the design. Continue punching along the edge of the paper.

④ Repeat for the remaining strips of paper. Use the diamond punch and the vellum strips to make continuous border punches along all of the edges, as in Steps 2 and 3.

⑤ Use the brush to apply liquid laminate to one side of the vase. Lay a strip of punched vellum onto the laminate, matching the top and bottom edges. Brush more laminate over the top to seal it down. Adhere the remaining two vellum strips down the sides of the vase, spacing them evenly. Let dry.

⑥ Use the laminate to adhere the strips of paper to the sides of the vase, staggering them between the vellum strips. Let dry.

⑦ Adhere the double-stick adhesive to the back of the foil. Cut each edge of the foil with the decorative-edge scissors. Measure and cut two pieces long enough to go around the vase with ⅛" overlap. Peel off the adhesive backing and wrap one piece around the top edge with the scallops about ½" onto the front. Fold the remaining foil over the inside of the vase. Repeat for the bottom of the vase, with the remaining foil folded onto the bottom of the vase.

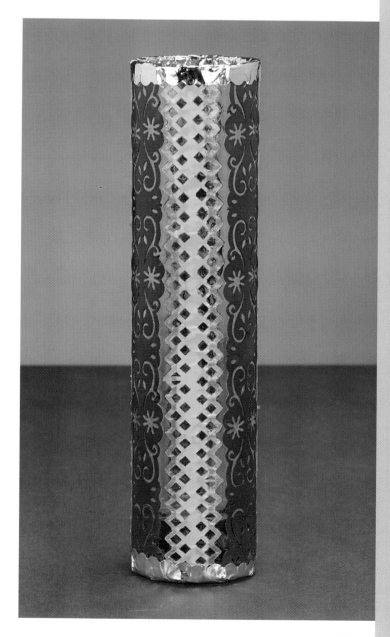

Wood-Burned and Painted Crate

From simple dots to an ornate pattern, there are many ways that wood burning and paint can enhance your floral arrangements. Try this pretty design on an otherwise ordinary wooden crate.

Designed by Jane Davis
Difficulty level: Intermediate

YOU WILL NEED

3" x 12" wooden container
Wood-burning tool
Paint, green
Oil colored pencils
Clear acrylic spray
Carbon paper and pencil, paintbrush

1 Trace the design onto the container. To make the design shown, mark the center of the container, then enlarge the pattern 200 percent on a photocopier. Use carbon paper to transfer the design to the container.

2 Using the wood burner, burn the lines of the design. Then, embellish as you choose, burning some lines darker, adding shading and dots or decorative lines.

3 When you are satisfied with the wood-burned design, add color with the oil color pencils.

4 Paint the edges of the container green. **Note:** If you accidentally get some paint on the sides of the wood, you can sand it away when the paint is dry.

5 Following the manufacturer's instructions, spray the completed project with a clear acrylic spray to seal the design and darken the wood color.

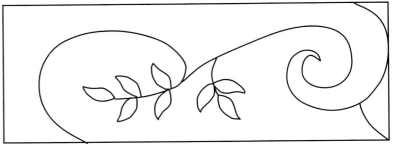

Bead Mosaic Terra Cotta Pots

Designed by Jane Davis
Difficulty Level: Easy

YOU WILL NEED

Small terra cotta pots
Variety of beads, all shapes, sizes, and colors, including long bugle beads, leaves, and flowers
Needle, toothpick, or tweezers
Clear acrylic spray (optional)
Newspaper or cardboard, pencil, tacky glue

These little pots can be complex or simple, depending on your taste and time. They are a great way to use beads from small to large, and can depict any season or scene.

Rosemary Pot

❶ Using a pencil, lightly write "Rosemary" along the rim of the pot.
❷ Squeeze a small amount of glue onto newspaper or cardboard.
❸ Pick up one bead at a time, dip the side of it in the glue, then place it on the pencil line on the pot. Repeat until all of the pencil lines are covered.
❹ For the plant, draw the basic stem lines on the pot, and glue bugle beads along the lines. Go back and glue more bugle beads at angles to the stems for the leaves. Glue small beads near the ends of the stems, between the leaves for flowers.
❺ If desired, spray the finished pot with a clear acrylic coating to preserve the design.

Decorated Rim

❶ Collect bugle beads of varying lengths and two types of seed beads.
❷ Working in the same way as the Rosemary pot, glue bugle beads all along the top of the rim. Let dry.
❸ Glue the other bugle beads along the rim, perpendicular to the first set of beads in the pattern shown on the finished pot.
❹ If desired, spray the finished pot with a clear acrylic coating to preserve the design.

Leaf and Posy Pot

❶ Place a small dot of glue just under the rim of the pot and let it set for about a minute. Press a leaf bead into the glue. Repeat around the rim.
❷ Glue flowers on the rim in the same way, with a leaf on either side of each flower.
❸ If desired, spray the finished pot with a clear acrylic coating to preserve the design.

Easy Etched Vase

Designed by Lisa Galvin
Difficulty level: Easy

Nothing looks as elegant on a glass vase as etching. Here's any easy way to achieve a store-bought look in very little time.

YOU WILL NEED

8½" square vase*
Etching crème*
Contact paper
Stainless steel sink or large plastic container
Alcohol (optional), dish soap, ink pen, lint-free cloth or coffee filter, ruler, scissors, water

*Used in this project: Syndicate Sales Square Vase; B & B Etching Products, Inc. etchall® etching crème.

1 Washing the vase with soap and water or alcohol. Dry with a lint-free cloth or coffee filter.

2 Cut the contact paper into 12 squares 1½" each, two strips 1½" x 7" each, and one piece 5" x 10". These will serve as your stencils.

3 One piece at a time, remove the paper backing and apply the contact paper as follows:

Apply three 1½" squares on all four sides, tilted like diamonds, so the points meet on two corners of the vase.

Apply the 1½" x 7" strips centered along the two opposite corners, meeting the opposite points of the diamonds.

Apply the 5" x 10" piece around the top of the exposed vase rim, overlapping the ends, with the excess extending above the vase.

Insert the excess portion of contact paper into the vase and press to the sides to protect the top and inside edges from coming in contact with the etching crème.

4 Using the squeegee provided with the etching crème, rub down all edges of the contact paper, removing any bubbles and/or air pockets. This will preven the etching crème from seeping beneath. Use the squeegee to apply a thick coat of etching crème to all sides, pulling the crème over the exposed surface as if you were icing a cake. Let stand for 15 minutes.

5 Remove the crème from the vase with the squeegee and return it to the bottle for re-use. Immediately rinse the etched surface to remove any remaining crème residue. Peel off the contact paper to reveal the finished design. The areas covered with contact paper are clear, while those exposed to etching crème are now permanently etched. Wash with soap and water.

Tips

Etchall® etching crème is reusable and can be returned to its container after etching to be used over and over again! You can use it to etch glass, mirrors, porcelain, ceramic, marble, and slate. It is important to note that etchall® etching crème will permanently etch all glazed and glass surfaces almost immediately. Avoid letting the crème touch any area that you do not want to etch, including porcelain sinks and tile countertops. Preferred containers for rinsing the small amount of crème residue left on a project when finished are plastic containers or a stainless steel sink. Objects etched with etchall® are dishwasher safe.

Metallic Vase

Designed by Kathy Kromer
Difficulty level: Easy

With little effort you can make this very contemporary vase!

YOU WILL NEED

Glass paint, blue and turquoise*
Looking glass paint kit*
Glass vase
Craft stick or pencil, newspapers,
    paper plates, paper towels

*Used in this project: Pebeo Vitrea 160 glass and crystal paint, Sapphire and Turquoise; Krylon Looking Glass paint kit.

1 Wash and dry the vase. Cover your work surface with newspaper.
2 Pour a small amount of the blue paint randomly around the inside of the vase. Let the paint drip down the inside of the vase. Repeat for the turquoise. Drip a little of both colors into the bottom of the vase. Tilt the vase until the colors cover the entire inside surface.
3 Turn the vase upside down on a paper plate to drain. Prop a craft stick or pencil under the vase so the paint can drain out. Let dry about one hour or until the paint no longer drains from the vase. Use paper towels to wipe away any paint on the outside of the vase. Let dry 24 hours.
4 In a well-ventilated area, follow the manufacturer's instructions to spray the inside of the vase. Let dry overnight, then spray with the sealer.

Polymer Clay Covered Container

Designed by Lisa Galvin
Difficulty level: Intermediate

This a great project for those who have never tried working with polymer clay before! The techniques are easy to do, yet promise to yield fabulous results!

YOU WILL NEED

4" galvanized topiary container
2 oz. packages of polymer clay, white and black*
Metallic finish, gold*
Cutting tool, bendable*
Brayer*
Permanent adhesive*
Assorted charms, metal findings, wire, and buttons of different textures, forms, and dimensions
Cookie sheet (for polymer clay use only), extra-fine sandpaper, old paintbrush, oven, pencil, ruler, scissors, tape, waxed paper, white paper

*Used in this project: AMACO; Fimo® Soft polymer clay, Rub 'n Buff® Metallic Finish in Grecian Gold, NuFlex Kato™ Blade, and Clay Roller; Beacon Adhesives Glass, Metal & More™ Premium Permanent Adhesive.

❶ With pencil, trace one side of the topiary container twice onto the paper to create two pattern pieces. On one pattern piece, draw a line about ¼" inside the pattern line, and cut out on this line. This will be used for cutting the black clay. Draw a line about ½" inside the pattern line on the second pattern piece, and cut out on this line. This will be used for cutting the white clay.

❷ Condition the polymer clay. Tape a piece of waxed paper to your work surface and roll the black with the brayer until it is about 1/16" thick. Place the larger pattern on the clay. Bend the cutting blade to cut one piece of clay, matching the pattern. Cut four pieces from black clay.

❸ Repeat Step 2 for the white clay, using the smaller pattern piece.

❹ Remove the black clay from the waxed paper and place each piece on the cookie sheet. Press various buttons, charms, metal findings, or wire into the outer edges of the clay, only far enough to leave an imprint of the form. Remove. Remove the white clay pieces from the waxed paper and center on top of the black clay, leaving only a border of the black visible around the white. Roll lightly to join the clay pieces together. Press the objects into the white clay, creating a "fossilized" faux-marble look.

❺ Bake the clay per the manufacturer's package instructions. Remove and let cool.

❻ Apply the gold finish to the top and outside edges of the clay. Using your finger or an old paintbrush, work the color into all grooves and indentations. Sand to remove the applied color from the raised portions of the clay, revealing only the impressions and creating an age-old appearance. **Note:** Be careful not to inhale any dust when sanding! Wipe away the dust with a damp paper towel and let dry.

❼ Glue the finished panels to each sides of the container. Let dry.

Working With Polymer Clay
Knead the clay. This will make the clay pliable, elastic, and easy to work with. Wash your hands prior to moving onto another color of clay to remove bits of clay and residue left on your hands and prevent discoloring other clay pieces.

Twig Container

Designed by Chris Malone
Difficulty level: Easy

Natural and earthy, branches and twigs of various shapes and sizes are a fun way to cover a plain container.

YOU WILL NEED

6½" square papier-mâché box
¼" to ⅝" diameter branches, straight, dry, and mostly straight*
1½ yds. mesh ribbon, natural
Spanish moss
3 small mushroom birds, green
Hand or power saw; hot glue gun and glue sticks

*About 50 were used for the sample shown.

❶ To determine the needed height of the branches, measure the height of the container and add 1". Cut the branches to size, leaving a few short forks for interest.
❷ Starting at one corner, glue the branches upright all around the papier-mâché box, varying diameters and straight and slightly bent. Leave at least one fork extending forward on the front.
❸ Wrap the mesh ribbon around the center of the box and tie it in a bow at the front corner. Gently pull on the loops to shape them.
❹ Glue a small bunch of Spanish moss to the fork on the front. Glue a bird in place in this "nest." Glue several additional bunches of moss around the container. Add the remaining birds as desired.

Embellished Skirt Container

Do you have old embellished linens in your closet or attic? Here's a great way to use them!

Designed by Chris Malone
Difficulty level: Easy

YOU WILL NEED

6½" tall round papier-mâché box
Fabric with embroidery, appliqué, or interesting print*
1½ yds. of 2" wide wire-edge ribbon to coordinate with fabric
Embellishments, such as buttons, buckles, charms, crocheted flowers, etc.
Acrylic paint, to coordinate with fabric
Fabric glue, foam paintbrush, ruler, scissors, sewing machine (optional), sewing thread

*You can use a pillowcase, table runner, or tablecloth; the sample shown is the front of an appliquéd and embroidered pillowcase.

1 Paint the outside and inside of the container.

2 Measure the container height and cut a decorated section of the fabric to that measurement plus 1¼" for the top hem. If a bottom hem needs to be sewn, add another ½". The width of the fabric skirt should be about one and one-half times the circumference of the container. If necessary, use the decorated section for the front and cut a matching piece for the back, sewing a seam at each side. Sew a double ¼" hem at the bottom, if needed.

3 Fold a 1¼" hem at the top. Sew gathering stitches 1" from the fold. Slip the skirt over the top of the container and pull the gathering threads to fit. Knot and clip the threads. Apply glue to the gathers on the wrong side to secure placement.

4 Wrap the ribbon around the skirt, covering the gathers. Tie it in a bow at the front. Tie a knot at each ribbon end and trim the ends in a V-cut. If using a buckle, as shown, thread the ribbon ends through it before tying in a bow. Glue the buttons and other embellishments on the ribbon on either side of the bow.

Painted Boot Container

Designed by Chris Malone
Difficulty level: Easy

YOU WILL NEED

Old lady's boot
Acrylic sealer/finisher*
Acrylic paint, country blue, dark pink, light and
    medium green, burgundy, cream, black
2 yds. 2½" wide ivory wire-edge ribbon
Compressed sponge, liner brush, 1 foam brush,
    palette, paper towels, scissors, small stencil brush,
    stylus or toothpick, tape

*Used in this project: DecoArt™ Americana™ Acrylic
Sealer/Finisher and Paint, Williamsburg Blue, Rasp-
berry, Jade Green, Hauser Medium Green, Deep
Burgundy, Light Buttermilk, Lamp Black

Revitalize an old boot with painted flowers and a lacy ribbon for the ties. Can't you just see ivy or another long piece of greenery trailing out of it?

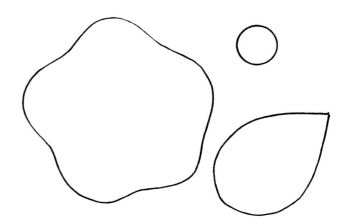

❶ Take the laces out of the boot and wash the boot with soap and water. Dry thoroughly.
❷ Spray the boot inside and out with two light coats of sealer.
❸ Paint the boot blue, including the tongue and top inside.
❹ Use the patterns to cut the flower, leaf, and polka-dot from the compressed sponge. To stamp with the sponge, dip it in water and squeeze to remove any excess water. Pour a puddle of paint on the palette and dip the sponge into the paint. Press onto the boot. Use the flower sponge to make four flowers with pink and the leaf sponge to make one or more leaves around each flower with light and medium green. Make random polka-dots with the small circle and cream paint.
❺ Dip the stencil brush in burgundy. Remove excess paint on the paper towel. Tap the brush to the flowers, near the edge, to add a little shading. In the same way, use cream paint in the center of each flower and lightly on each leaf.
❻ Thin the black slightly with water. Use the liner brush to paint wiggly outlines around each flower and leaf. Use the stylus or toothpick to make random block dots on the flowers and leaves. When all paint is dry, finish with two light coats of sealer.
❼ Lace the boots with ribbon (tape the ribbon ends if necessary to facilitate the lacing). Tie a bow at the top of the boot. Tie a knot at each end and trim ends in a V-cut.
❽ To use the boot for fresh flowers, insert a plastic or glass container inside before lacing the boot with ribbon.

Stamped Terra Cotta Pots

Choose any rubber stamp image you'd like to embellish these delightful pots.

Designed by Lauren Johnston
Difficultly level: Easy

YOU WILL NEED

Small oak leaf rubber stamp, solid and outline*
Terra cotta pots and saucers
Rubber stamp pads, black, dark and light green, red*
Gloss sealer*
Pen, black*
Foam brush, heat gun

*Used in this project: Duets Oak Leaf Stamp; Crafter's®
Option Plate Pads®; Krylon Triple-Thick Crystal Clear Glaze;
Zig Dotta-riffic Pen.

1 Ink the solid image leaf stamp with dark green or red and stamp onto the pot. Do not worry if the images do not come out perfect. The black outline image will help to hide any mistakes.

2 Continue to stamp around the pot, alternating the greens, if desired.

3 Apply black ink to the outline stamp. Stamp over the solid leaves.

4 Use the heat gun to heat-set each stamped image for approximately 1 to 2 minutes.

5 Use the black pen to make large dots randomly around the rim, as desired.

6 For the saucers, dab on ink around the outside edges and heat-set. Fill in the extra spaces with dots.

7 After the pots and saucers are dry, brush with several coats of gloss sealer.

Enameled Crate

Create the interesting texture on this crate with any rubber stamp you'd like.

Designed by Lauren Johnston
Difficulty level: Easy

YOU WILL NEED

Embossing enamel, gold, bronze, clear*
Wood crate
Pigment stamp pad, gold*
Embossing stamp pad, clear*
Heat tool
Rubber stamp of your choice
Spray paint, gold metallic*

*Used in this project: Ultra Thick Embossing Enamel™ (UTEE); ColorBox® Pigment Stamp Pad, Gold; Top Boss® Embossing Stamp Pad, Clear; Krylon Spray Paint, Gold Metallic.

❶ Spray all sides of the crate with gold paint. Let dry.
❷ Working one section at a time, dab on a generous coat of gold pigment ink and sprinkle with gold embossing enamel. Heat with the heat tool until the enamel is melted. Continue until the front and side panels are enameled.
❸ Ink the rubber stamp with clear embossing ink; set aside.
❹ For the next layer of enamel, dab the clear embossing ink one section at a time, and sprinkle with clear embossing enamel and a small amount of bronze embossing enamel. Heat until the enamel is molten, and immediately impress the inked stamp into the enamel. Leave it there until the enamel hardens (it only takes a few seconds).
❺ Continue this process in sections until all areas have two layers and have been stamped.

Weddings For All Seasons
*90+ Ways to Personalize
Your Wedding*
by Krause Publications

Your wedding day is a very important day in your life and can be one of the most expensive. This complete book of wedding crafts will show you how to make a wide variety of projects, suitable for any time of the year, that will make your day an unforgettable, yet affordable, occasion. Dozens of unique projects cover everything you need for a bridal shower, reception, the wedding day, and after. Make it a day to remember!

Softcover • 8-1/4 x 10-7/8 • 128 pages
150 color photos
Item# MWED • $18.95

French-Beaded Flowers
New Millennium Collection
by Dalene Kelly

Learn to make beautiful floral works of art with this popular beading technique. Author Dalene Kelly will guide you with step-by-step instructions to make 38 different flowers, such as tiger lilies, trilliums, pansies, irises, and gladiolas. You will then learn how to incorporate these unique flowers into four creative projects — a cymbidium corsage, rose hair barrette, Shasta daisy napkin ring, and rose bud bridal veil.

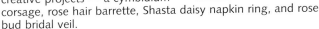

Softcover • 8-1/4 x 10-7/8 • 96 pages
55 color photos, 40+ illustrations
Item# FREBD • $18.95

Cindy Walter's Snippet Sensations Bouquets
by Cindy Walter

Creating art with fabric has never been so fun and easy! In Cindy Walter's new book, you'll be introduced to her revolutionary Snippet Sensations technique, where "snippets" of fabric and fusible web are used to "paint" on fabric. You'll then be guided with step-by-step instructions through 10 stunning floral projects that can be quilted, including a sunflower quilt.

Softcover • 8-1/4 x 10-7/8 • 24 pages
30 color photos
Item# SNBQT • $7.95

The Secrets of Fashioning Ribbon Flowers
*Heirlooms For the
Next Generation*
by Helen Gibb

What to do with all that gorgeous ribbon available today? Easy, fashion the most elegant flowers imaginable. Incorporate 15 different flowers into jewelry, home decor, wearables, and more. Included are instructions for making the leaves, calyx, and stems.

Softcover • 8-1/4 x 10-7/8 • 128 pages
150 b&w Illustrations • 100 color photos
Item# FFFGD • $24.95

Glorious Ribbons
by Christine Kingdom

Weave it. Pleat it. Fold it. Then try embroidery and appliqué — all with ribbon. Bows, baskets, roses, garlands and 50 other projects provide you with hours of crafting pleasure and fill your home with affordable accents and exquisitely personal touches.

Softcover • 8-1/4 x 10-7/8
128 pages
Color throughout
Item# GLRI • $19.95

Character Wreaths
by Kasey Rogers & Mark Wood

Learn how to create 20 different character wreaths to decorate your home for every season and various holidays. Includes easy-to-follow instructions and great photographs to guide you through each project. Rogers and Wood are also the authors of *Halloween Crafts: Eerily Elegant Décor* and Rogers played Louise Tate on the classic TV show *Bewitched*.

Softcover • 8-1/4 x 10-7/8
48 pages
50 color photos
Item# CHAWR • $10.95

To order call
800-258-0929 Offer CRB2

Krause Publications
Offer CRB2
P.O. Box 5009
Iola WI 54945-5009
www.krausebooks.com

Shipping & Handling: $4.00 first book, $2.25 each additional. Non-US addresses $20.95 first book, $5.95 each additional.

Sales Tax: CA, IA, IL, NJ, PA, TN, VA, WI residents please add appropriate sales tax.